A Pocket Full of God

Also by David Knight

Pathway

Pathway (2nd Edition)

Deliverance of Love, Light and Truth

I am I: The In-Dweller of Your Heart

I am I: The In-Dweller of Your Heart (Part 2)

I am I: The In-Dweller of Your Heart (Part 3)

I am I: The In-Dweller of Your Heart 'Collection'

Leave the Body Behind

A POCKET FULL OF GOD

Transform the Nature of Your Life

By David Knight

'A Pocket Full of God'
Copyright © 2020 by DPK Publishing/AscensionForYou.

All rights reserved.

ISBN: 978-1-8380091-0-6
eISBN: 978-1-8380091-1-3

Without limiting the rights under copyright reserved above, no part of this publication may be reproduced, stored in or introduced into a retrieval system, or transmitted, in any form, or by any means (electronic, mechanical, photocopying, recording, or otherwise) without the prior written permission of both the copyright owner and the above publisher of this book.

This book is sold subject to the condition that it shall not, by way of trade or otherwise, be lent, resold, hired out, or otherwise circulated without the publisher's prior consent in any form of binding or cover other than that in which it is published and without a similar condition including this condition being imposed on the subsequent purchaser. Under no circumstances may any part of this book be photocopied for resale.

A CIP catalogue record for this book is available from the British Library.

Cover layout by Curious Cat Books

www.ascensionforyou.com

Contents

Foreword 7

Introduction 9

Chapter 1 ....
I Will Lift Your Heart 13

Chapter 2 ....
Silence is the Speech of the Spiritual Seeker . 23

Chapter 3 ....
Self-Realisation & Liberation 33

Chapter 4 ....
Divinity 49

Chapter 5 ....
Karma 63

Chapter 6 ....
Love and Light 71

Chapter 7 ....
Health and Wealth 95

Chapter 8 ....
Religion and Belief ... Faith and Trust 101

Chapter 9 ....
Body, Mind and Soul 109

Chapter 10 ....
Your Physical and Non-Physical Journey ... 121

Afterword 157

Bibliography 159

About the Author 165

Glossary – Spiritual Guidance and Education..167

An invitation from David Knight......................194

If you enjoy reading *A Pocket Full of God*, you can download *Deliverance of Love, Light, and Truth* for free, when you join David's mission for a 'full and blissful life'.

To learn more, visit: www.ascensionforyou.com

Foreword

"This vision that reads these words isn't owed to me. It could be taken at any moment, but for this moment, I get to enjoy it. Only for now do I get to see beauty. Any beauty I see in the future is a gift.

This food I eat isn't owed to me. Mother Earth could have kept it for herself, and maybe one day she will choose to, but for this moment, she shares it with me. Only for now do I get to eat. Any food I have in the future is a gift.

This next breath isn't owed to me. The trees that give their oxygen may not always be here, but for this moment, the trees and I share our breath with each other so that we each may live. Only for now am I being granted this exchange of life. Any breath I have (to give and receive) in the future is a gift. Thank you. Thank you. Thank you."

When something is 'lost' it can serve as a reminder that it was never really 'yours' to begin with. Everything on this plane of existence is temporary. So, a 'loss' can be a prompt to experience gratitude for what you still have. I invite you to reflect on the many gifts you've been able to "borrow" during your life.

- Derek Deopker

Introduction

We are sparks of God, the Divine, the Creator ... and every life form throughout the Cosmos exists only because the same Universal energy flows through them all.

When you acknowledge and understand this fact (along with a constant inner enquiry to our true connection), you become your own teacher of truth.

Comprehend that silence and stillness allow you to venture beyond the boundary of the senses. And, by turning inwards, you harness an innate ability to rise above the restrictive process of one's thoughts and emotions ... which evolve from past impressions upon the mind and countless experiences of the body.

Appreciate that it is here and here alone where you may utilize the intelligence of your consciousness towards the goal of eternal bliss.

This will provide you with a continual opportunity to bear witness to your union with Creation, and help you bypass (or even erase) your karmic memory built over the eons of time.

A Pocket Full of God

To aid you further towards your transformation, these short passages of knowledge (from the eternal sea of wisdom) have been accumulated over many hours of meditative and internal contemplation.

The Spiritual guidance and education they contain can be your constant companion, a true friend that does not judge, but who remains a helping hand as you make your way along the path of life.

May these reflections from the heart assist you by bringing clarity to the mind and the contentment and freedom from the attachments of the world around you.

They will also confirm you possess the capability to transcend the limitations of the physical and become receptive to many dimensions and forms of energy ... and liberation from all forms of ignorance.

Remember, as Derek mentioned in the foreword, everything is temporary. You are mortal and have a limited amount of time here, and no one knows when your life will be over.

So, when you embark upon the challenges ahead, try to be conscious in all your actions ... and believe that what you do and achieve in work and rest or play brings progress, not only for yourself but for humanity and planet Earth too.

Introduction

Re-learn to be joyful—unaffected by what you may deem as the good or bad of anything. Finally, please have fun ... for you already reside in a heavenly realm of love and light!

Chapter 1

I Will Lift Your Heart

I will lift your heart when you are sad, and I will smile and laugh with you when delight passes through your soul's journey ... so do not fear, for I am always nearer than near. Then, by acknowledging the statement, 'I am you and you are me', we become the true tree of life, for I live through the words on your lips, the sights you see, the pain and joy and every experience and moment you were, are, and can be.

Know I am:

The boat, which carries you across the ocean(s) of your emotions.

The land you walk upon, holding you upright and true.

The wind, to blow dark clouds away from your mind, body, and soul.

The spiritual 'vision' to reveal the light, and

the Sun to radiate warmth and love within.

The hand that lifts you up from the ground when you feel you cannot go on.

The life-giving 'water', to quench your thirst for truth, knowledge, and wisdom.

The spark deep within you, which gives you everlasting life.

The colours of the rainbow, shining down upon your darkened days of false fears and tears.

※ ※ ※

This day can be the start of something new and brilliant, which changes your life and those around you forever. Each day forthwith can be lived like it was your last, with meaning and justification, one of hope and glory and most importantly … joy. Only you can limit love, which emanates from the kindness and peace pouring from the heart and Soul.

※ ※ ※

Believe you are strong, stronger than you can ever possibly imagine. No building, barrier or even a confused mind can contain your truth and Divinity and soul.

Therefore, you are not trapped, caged, or

I Will Lift Your Heart

controlled by any such things in a material world, because your true 'self' is already free to soar as high and far as one's will allows. If you are ever in doubt or think you are alone, turn inward to discover the reality of you.

✺ ✺ ✺

Just as the Sun's rays bathe the Earth with light and warmth, so does my Divinity, which glistens and radiates for every form of life-energy.

With the wind, my breath washes over your face. Through the water you drink, I satisfy your thirst. Within the soil, I cultivate nutrients for your body. Inside your heart, I am the love that beats fast or slow, to lead and guide and will you to grow and know your true self … a fragment of creation with the same power to create.

✺ ✺ ✺

Whenever you are 'still', you will recognise me as the air that fills your lungs … the breath of life. As sunshine falls upon your face, know I am here, there and am forever in every place.

Should you hear bird song (like a gentle lullaby), realise I am within you always, never to say good-bye. When you smell the fragrance from colourful blooms and petals, understand I am the only scent perfuming all 'life'.

By bearing witness to spectacular and natural phenomena, know your gaze has seen but a fragment of my power. If you touch and wipe a tear from your eye, appreciate your soul bleeds the truth of your reality that is both you and 'I'.

✵ ✵ ✵

Your own appearance in this world can state more than a thousand words or 'scenes'. Your heart and smile can inspire and shine far greater than those who appear to be in the limelight and obtain what some describe as false glory.

So, you do not need a medal or an Oscar for me to recognise your true worth. In all walks of life, the simple act of one's performance is enough ... if you try your utmost to become the best person and joyful soul you can be.

✵ ✵ ✵

I am forever your friend and confidant and your rock to cling to when all else seems lost around you. Appreciate I am the light within the darkness, and the helping hand to raise you from the ground when you fall to your knees.

I Will Lift Your Heart

Know that I will quench your thirst for knowledge and guide you to the wisdom you require too. With words to encourage and inspire you, I remain the comforting arm during tears of grief or the stranger who materialises during desperate times.

Understand there is always an answer; a way out of the debris and fallout when the emotional storm appears to engulf you in your life.

Life is what you make it, and even in troubled times, I am there, if you look for me. I am the smile, the birdsong, and the lone flower amongst the weeds of discontent, hurt and anger. I am the softly spoken who assists you in the hour of need … yes, I am the light and am all things in all places.

Remember, if your heart appears to have taken you as far as it will go, then do not fear and worry or shed tears of pain or anguish, because accepting my strength with genuine conviction can help you achieve your dreams!

Your reality was not born but is everything that ever was and shall be. Therefore, if doubt and fear are a weakness, I will make you strong. By conquering false emotions, you break free from the confusion and illusion, to find immortality beyond the boundary of the physical. Remember, be still in love and light.

❇ ❇ ❇

You can be the rainbow which illuminates other hearts, or the water to satisfy the thirst of another. You can nourish the unfortunate and can provide warmth, shelter, care, and reassurance in innumerable ways to your fellow 'man'.

❇ ❇ ❇

Today can be the starting point for you to pick yourself up and dust yourself down. Arise now from the comfort zone of any pride or selfishness … to display the love which shines from and through and to you without end.

Over time, all thoughts and actions will become selfless. By showing compassion and helping any other life form, you make offerings of love and joy to me. This is the true sacrifice, not of fear, hurt or death, but one placed upon the altar of my heart, to be remembered forever and a day.

✠ ✠ ✠

There are many who sit or walk seemingly alone, who appear neglected by their kith and kin, society, country and even humanity. For those I speak of, understand I am with you every step you take. And know this; I hold your hand while every heart is placed inside my own.

I cradle you within my grace, which I pour over your souls to eternally sustain you. Whilst you may often believe the world has abandoned you, realise you are not (and can never be) a stranger to me, as we are forever 'one'.

✠ ✠ ✠

For those without a bed (whether through one's own karma and experience), you shall lie down in my fields of peace. The fragrance of my love will raise thy hearts to magical planes of bliss beyond the fear and dread of the night and cold.

As for the emptiness of 'belly', please understand this is only temporary. Know you will be fulfilled inside and out, by simply accepting that you already sit at my table within the Kingdom of Heaven … to be nourished by trust, an unwavering faith, and with the realisation of our oneness … ecstasy.

※ ※ ※

Do not be dismayed or disturbed by lists of things to accomplish, problems to solve, people to meet and places to go, or by the inconvenient noise made by people and other impermanent things.

Where you can, try to de-clutter the mental horizon by focusing on nature, and those natural sounds about you, like birdsong, insects buzzing and the rustling of leaves.

Alternatively, if you should open your eyes, gaze out of the window towards passing clouds and birds in flight, or to the butterflies and bees resting upon nearby flowers.

You could even go outside to sense the sunshine on your face, for it will surely lift your spirit, and cast many burdens from your shoulders.

※ ※ ※

Become conscious of the reality of our union … because I am the warmth if you are cold. I am the drink to quench your thirst. I am the light when you are blinded by darkness. I am the land encircling the ocean of doubt. I am the sky and clouds drifting by, watching over you. I am the mountain you climb in earnest, to eventually reach the peak, seemingly alone … yet entwined within my heart you will be. I am the perfume of sweetness from a flower. I am the air that fills your lungs. I am the touch caressing your face in a loving embrace. Indeed, I am everything and everything I am.

I will never leave you and always help you. By turning inward, you take one step towards me. My presence will seem closer to thee, until one day you realise you are already 'home' … to reside in the permanence of light, this I promise.

Remember, by discovering the truth 'within', you will recognise beauty beyond all things; it is no mystery, as there is only you.

Chapter 2

Silence is the Speech of the Spiritual Seeker

Feel, sense, and acknowledge me in the grass, flowers, trees, rivers, seas, mountains, sky, fire, earth, and space beyond. Realise me within the stillness inside yourself, for here I reside with (and for) you, to guide you towards eternal bliss.

※ ※ ※

In the stillness of solitude and contemplation, you hear me though I do not speak. You know me inside your heart, though I am unknowable to the mind. You sense me as a memory or a thought, a longing for something more. Now feel my love like the warmth from a protective blanket, which envelopes you like a cocoon—an unbreakable shell until ascension from the physical and impermanent plane.

One's spiritual guidance and education are a gradual process for some, but for others, it pierces like a lightning bolt through their world and the way they live their lives.

Appreciate your eyes will truly open to seeing life from a new perspective and therefore you will feel different within your being. It will captivate you and tug your heartstrings. Tears will flow, and your emotional relief and joy will enter your thoughts and words and deeds, because you will be 'refreshed' on a soul level.

One must consciously and continually take yourself to the subtle, for through our connection you will find the answers and freedom you crave and seek.

Here, your spark and Divine essence can become brighter and clearer every day if you wish it to. In fact, the flame of love and light inside you shall bloom like a flower, and its petals will glisten and shimmer … more beautiful than the stars that shine on the darkest of nights. Please know that your love is sweeter than nectar, and more fragrant than any field of majestic and radiant flowers too.

Silence is the Speech of the Spiritual Seeker

In stillness and peace, you sense my presence, because you are separated from the clutter inside your mind and everything else that envelops the body. Here, I wrap you in my love ... which is my gift, my present, pre-sent during the eternal dawn of awakening. Be soothed by gentle lullabies and the sound of two hearts beating as one. I empower you with all that I am, so you can become 'realised', to know what you are destined to be ... your 'true self'.

Sit in silence and become elevated beyond the false image of what you currently think of as 'you' ie. the body. Now comprehend all that you are ... life-energy in its truest form —'light'. Then, you will resonate through and upon higher frequencies and dimensions, and new understanding will flow like water over rock, cascading from energy points around your form through many chakras to stabilise your very being. New knowledge shall provide you with the wisdom one requires, by living the experience of 'man' and so much more besides.

You think you are infinitesimal, but beyond the mind, you will realise you are everything and everything is you. Belief brings balance. Through wisdom comes the understanding every soul is a brilliant light which becomes more beautiful by being cleansed from its journey through time.

All shall value this process and dimension as it helps to remove the dust and debris of past thoughts and deeds ... which prevented one's own illumination from being discovered through your many previous bodily incarnations and life experiences.

When you become quiet and sit in stillness, you feel my presence. Peace, tranquillity, and my love not only impress upon your earthly senses, but you also start to appreciate this inside your heart and soul.

Your everlasting light shall sparkle even brighter through you (and back unto me) for it shines eternal. In truth, no amount of darkness, decay or negativity can ever erase who and what you are—a spark of my Divinity.

Silence is the Speech of the Spiritual Seeker

Your thought process often tries to disguise the truth from you, and as such, you sometimes imagine you are on your own, separate from me, but you are not alone and can never be.

Unlike a lost memory of a forgotten name or face, you will want to remember who and what you truly are, because searching for answers (in silence) will lead you towards self-realisation. Then, within your heart, you comprehend life is more than a simple daily 'existence'; and the 'eureka' moment will not be too far away.

People may experience tiny nuggets of spiritual knowledge in a variety of ways, often through the expression and creativity of the spoken word or via books and films etcetera. However, only by tapping into their heart of love and light can they appreciate that it is here and here alone where the unwavering certainty of truth will sink deep within their core. Eventually, wisdom follows the acceptance of the one true miracle … the undying beauty, bliss, and Nirvana of our oneness.

When our connection manifests itself inside you, it transcends into thought and right action, which ensures a positive outcome. Within this process, forgiveness and compassion soon trickle through as love, which will shine like a beacon and sparkle like a brilliant star.

Being rekindled by your own reality allows you to embrace, foster and share this light. And, humanity connecting in truth becomes radiant and magical, to be cast upon my breath as stardust, sprinkled across time, space and all dimensions.

✖ ✖ ✖

If you remain focused, the existence of our totality will not become a snapshot of what came to pass. Unlike an old photograph buried in an album of so-called treasured moments, it is you who 'captured' me.

✖ ✖ ✖

Therefore, the soul can bloom with the fragrance of love, and though your body changes every day in some way, I am the one constant, the reminder and true picture which you can continue to develop in truth.

Silence is the Speech of the Spiritual Seeker

When your truth is revealed, connecting directly with your soul, you will know and feel it ... like a hand in a glove or your feet in well-worn shoes. Instant recognition proves they belong to you and you to them, they are a perfect fit ... comfortable, without resistance or restriction, which brings a sense of wholeness.

Each soul requires protection, guidance, truth and light, and the strength and peace which brings this stability are not in any sacred building, a so-called safe house or stronghold—it is within you!

This true fortitude and fortress can withstand every test because the foundations are built of love. Pillars of faith and hope support your whole being, and these enable your mind to repel negative traits, discontent, and desire if you just embrace and let them do so.

If you are unable to reflect and contemplate in silence, feel me as the wind or sunshine upon your face, and the raindrops falling on your cheek. Sense me in the perfume of a flower ... and realise me as the mountains, valleys and seas, or the stars and far off galaxies.

Wonder of me as birds fly and the animals roam through the beauty of the land too, but even if you gaze far and wide, only through searching 'within' do you see the reality and so much more.

Please try to understand and appreciate, everything you think, and experience is but a fragment, a minute atom of all that I am, and of what you are too.

※ ※ ※

By being 'still' your inner child becomes free, and you loosen those constraints created by your own mind and nothing can hold you back. In fact, there is no place in existence where you cannot go or soul's presence you cannot feel or see. You can achieve anything through the ethereal realm of energy and love ... if it resonates within peace and truth.

So, you must seek the 'goal' from inside you, as this is the only way to succeed. You will not find your answers in any other human being as every embodiment, no matter how loving, how peaceful, or how beautiful, has their own karma to balance and their own life and road to follow.

Silence is the Speech of the Spiritual Seeker

Therefore, by taking time out from the hustle and bustle of your daily tasks to contemplate in silence, you will find the pause for breath can be an elixir of life.

Indeed, with the mind disengaged from self-induced worry, your heart can open to feel my presence, and therefore a restless Spirit becomes a restful one.

Now, let us take flight together as you are my other wing. We will soar higher and further than you ever thought or dreamt possible. You can never fly too near the Sun as love's rays only beckon you to shine more intensely and brightly (each day or lifetime) than you have ever done before. Some may say the sky is the limit, but in truth, it is not even the start. Understand, deep within you; our love is for eternity … forever, world without end.

Chapter 3

Self-Realisation & Liberation

What is the real destination of your heart & soul? Through self-realisation, you will lose your immorality and become a true being of human values and radiate love, kindness, compassion, forgiveness and truth. These are the stepping-stones across the waters of doubt and fear which guide you to my heart forevermore. Immortality of the soul is the reality, but it is in the recognition and understanding of such which leads you towards the goal.

Energy and love and intellect are my Creation, and Creation is life.

Please comprehend the glory of the truth was with you in the beginning and perpetually stays through you whenever and wherever you reside.

Time, distance and every level of vibration (sound/energy) and dimension make no difference either because love is whole, it is Universal and all-powerful and forms 'Creation' itself. It is for everyone. All you need to do is to recognise this through the realisation of the self, by simply remembering and becoming who and what you truly are.

✠ ✠ ✠

I urge you to sense me and know me as the Universe and the whole of Creation, forever growing and expanding beyond your mind and dreams.

Please understand, when I breathe, the life force and energy of love flow through my beating heart into every fibre, particle, atom, and every element known or unknown to mankind.

✠ ✠ ✠

For one to progress, take a step towards me ... and to achieve what you think is impossible, take three. Subsequently, try to push aside those clouds of doubt by remembering to live inside my heart as 'one', and thereby remove any

Self-Realisation & Liberation

confusion or feelings of separateness to each other.

In silence, you will find the truth, and the spiritual 'seeker' knows that through their experience comes the real expression of our love as 'one'. By feeling and acknowledging this connection each day, your acceptance of your own reality can grow stronger, and in turn, this will enable you to express yourself in your true light.

Your sojourn (soul-journey) needs only one route to follow, and this 'inner' path is each your own. Hence, no written word, guru or Saint can walk it for you, and neither would you wish them to.

As a result, if you see, hear or imagine there is a quick fix, a secret and worldly explanation or any other magical formulae which states you can access the truth by any other means than through thy heart—then they are sorely mistaken.

Understand, only you can make this judgment call by accepting what does or does not resonate inside you … in the knowledge I will never be your judge and jury because you are forever your own.

※ ※ ※

Good day, or moreover a 'God' day to you. Understand that the time you set aside to be 'still' becomes the bridge and connection of eternal love.

Therefore, please try not to worry as you walk upon the path called 'life', even if the road seems rough and demanding on your body and mind. This may test your faith and cause you to believe in our separation when there is none. There is only unity ... and all have equal parity upon their quest and journey.

※ ※ ※

When you are in this stillness, one could say I am 'happy'. By sensing me, the Stars appear brighter and your hearts sparkle more beautiful than all the diamonds and so-called prized jewels of the world.

These moments are unforgettable, etched within your soul's memories forever and a day, and no earthly price can ever be placed upon them.

Self-Realisation & Liberation

✠ ✠ ✠

Comprehend, it is your true self which is the greatest discovery of all. You do not need to travel or go anywhere else to find this truth! You are the miracle, the be-all and end-all ... and yet you were, are and forever will be without a 'beginning' to meet no 'end'.

Just as light expands eternally throughout Creation, so does love and life-energy inside you too... but you must acknowledge and accept this reality within because it is all-sustaining and pervading.

✠ ✠ ✠

I am limitless and will not be a 'keeper', refusing or denying you what you seek. I am not an 'only for tomorrow' God either. Ultimately, through self-realisation, you will understand this within your soul. You just need to believe the truth of you, so love can manifest and pour forth like water over rock, eroding ego, and any disdain for your fellow man.

✠ ✠ ✠

Do not fret or imagine I am angry in any way, shape, or form, because I am not ... I only wish for you to realise the 'oneness' of all things. Know that a friend, neighbour, community, and country is one and whole without division or separation.

As such, the energy of life resides in every flower, rock, mountain, river, sea and all things ... and when you clear the fear and illusion away from the physical eyes, (and the mind which plays tricks is subdued), you can sense everything is 'me'.

Indeed, every petal, snowflake, tree, all animals and insects and each drop of an ocean's water are ingredients of my Divinity... and so they are yours too!

When you realise and believe your true boundless state of being and energy exists, it becomes easier to comprehend and acknowledge you are already free with the same power to mould the way you think, feel and live. You possess the ability to bend, shape and create the life you deserve (inside and out) because you are Creation, not separate from it.

You co-create through 'self', with each other, and through me too. Therefore, place trust in yourself to reach your full potential as a human being and soul.

Self-Realisation & Liberation

Each person can achieve their heart's desire and make their ultimate dream come true, but will you? By keeping me near and dear, and by wishing to know the truth then I remain a reflection of those wishes. Remember, I am not distant from you, so why would you want to try and distance yourself from me? I am not just behind, in front of, or beside you … I am inside you because I am you. By recognising me … you will simply recognise yourself.

In stillness, you can understand the difference between the exterior world with its influences and impermanent desires, and the true Creation where bliss and love reign supreme. In your hectic life, one must wonder if you betray yourself, making up reasons or excuses not to connect with your own heart.

Remember, there is the unique opportunity to attain self-realisation and liberation of this age, so at what point do you start to comprehend this truth and believe in who and what you are and why you exist.

Each one of you has the ability and freedom

within to do so. This basic choice places the onus upon the 'individual' ... to move forward and become brighter and lighter and fulfil their true potential of bliss and peace.

※ ※ ※

By being 'still' you will hear me, for your heartbeat and rhythm blends with mine as one. Here, the understanding will reveal itself if you believe it to be so.

Hence, do not search for answers in transient, exterior, and impermanent things, they will only deceive you with a false thirst for passing pleasures, and these will drain your material and emotional resources.

※ ※ ※

Accepting mercy within your life guides you forward, enabling you to see this 'present', a golden nugget of your growth; spiritually, mentally, and emotionally. This shall lead you towards unconditional love and drive away any last traces of fear lingering inside your heart or mind.

It also provides you with a renewed hope and vigour, to achieve those ambitions and fulfil the dreams you strive to embark upon. Remember

Self-Realisation & Liberation

though, only the self-realisation through your soul can reveal the real 'treasure' at the end of the rainbow.

I do not imply you should live a pauper's life and hideaway in a remote cave or even deny yourself comforts of the body ... only that you should try to be content, especially when your senses attempt to deceive and trick you. Worse still, if they actively lead you to cause pain upon another person, animal or any being.

Appreciate you are given what you need, and not what you think you want. This way, you can move forward in trust, with belief and the knowledge everything is as it should be.

From here, you can reach beyond the stars, because in, through, from, and to love, the sky has no limits ... without any bodily limitations imposed upon you at all.

In fact, you are boundless, like the cosmos ... but you must first awake and emerge from the bubble of your sub-conscious to realise it.

This voyage of discovery you have embarked upon does not leave the dock to reach a new port, as you constantly reside upon the sea of truth.

Understand, I am not the stowaway who wants to be ignored, but I am I ... the 'Indweller', who can always help you, no matter where you go.

Know I am not the Captain either, who barks orders to make you comply and control you. However, if you merely allow me, I will be the sail upon a mast and a ship's wheel and rudder ... as my aim is to guide, lead, encourage and support you in every endeavour.

In addition, our oneness ensures I can do this if you only realise you are the vessel and I am the true power of your magnificence.

Then, by keeping faith in our unity, you will retain a real belief, for not only will you trust me ... but also those actions you deem are your own.

✠ ✠ ✠

Your physical being (which is almost entirely made of water) can float, bob, and weave, as well as rise and fall upon the sea of emotions. You may travel by all modes of transport, but when stripped bare to your Divine essence, you

Self-Realisation & Liberation

simply merge as a wave upon my ocean of love.

※ ※ ※

When you believe in yourself, you can appreciate I am your mast and the sails which carry you along to where you belong, so you are not lost, not to me.

And, if you somehow feel doubtful of my love, or become disorientated by a whirlpool of desire through the impermanent world, reach for our connection inside your heart and I will instantly bring you to safer, calmer waters.

※ ※ ※

One's destiny is to reach the shore of truth, and by removing your anger, which is the anchor of confusion and illusion weighing you down, you will soon comprehend your self-realisation will lead you towards the goal. No longer will you sail across the rivers of doubt, which always attempt to keep you from knowing your true 'self', and me.

※ ※ ※

Like a flotilla of ships, each of you appears diverse in looks and appearance, but you can all undertake the journey of self-realisation without any trepidation or prejudice. Indeed, all vessels may be carrying flags which display different nationalities or to show they are affiliated to various religions or faiths, or even those who carry the skull and crossbones to induce fear or death.

Know there are some who can even temporarily travel away from the light, but as I see all things, there is no darkness or any depths which can disguise or hide a soul from me.

One day, every 'body' will comprehend their true direction and purpose, it is only a matter of time. After all, each ship has their anchor endlessly attached to my heart, and therefore you can never be lost or cast adrift but will forever sail with me throughout time and space and every dimension of existence.

You are each a feather, which forms a 'wing' upon the dove of peace. Our love is the other

Self-Realisation & Liberation

wing ... which enables you to take flight and fulfil your destiny.

✠ ✠ ✠

Fly high, higher than you thought or believed was possible. Discover the reality and our unity in the silence of your heart, and all your dreams will come true.

✠ ✠ ✠

Controlling the lower 'self' re-ignites the power, passion, and determination of your higher 'self'. No person can do this for another, as each one of you must make your own choice and decision. Night and day, different time zones, minutes, hours, weeks, months, or years bear little or no relevance here.

✠ ✠ ✠

As stated earlier, I am I, the In-dweller of your heart, and in recognising me you will finally recognise your own self. For now, these are just words; but when you delve into your own divine essence, you'll discover a richness of purity, light and peace which can never be erased, broken, burnt or buried so deeply that you can ever lose sight of the truth again.

�✹ ✹ ✹

Some people may think that because I am the Creator/Creation—omnipotent, omnipresent, and omniscient—that I could not want or wish for anything. They are mistaken. If you are a spark of me, I long for you to return to the flame.

You, as a soul also resemble a grain of sand, and only when the sea of emotion returns you to rest upon the shore of tranquillity am I forever whole.

Your hearts are the real jewels scattered throughout the Universe, and only when every single one recognises who and what they truly are will the glory of my name be fulfilled.

Therefore, I long and pain for you to comprehend the reality and truth of 'you' … far away from the lies and deceit within the bondage of death and rebirth.

✹ ✹ ✹

Okay then, where do you go from here? Well, you could think about who, what and why 'you are who you are' because, for all that is said and

Self-Realisation & Liberation

done, there is a role for you to fulfil.

So, please do not merge into the background of your surroundings in the attempt to disguise yourself like a chameleon (which changes colour through anguish or fear) and remain anonymous amongst your kith and kin.

Understand I do not chastise you or expect you to find fulfilment through temporary accolades, medals, and awards either … but urge and wish you to strive for the greatest prize of all, self-realisation into bliss and peace.

I accept your strength and your weaknesses.
I accept your kindness and devotion.
I accept your pathways which each one of you take.
I accept your Love and Light too.
And…
I am the shoreline and your safe harbour.
I am the firm and smooth ground you walk upon.
I am the air you breathe.
I am the Sun that warms your face.
I am the hope of your change.
I am the faith which burns away doubt.
I am the tears that melt your heart.
I am the attainable dream of bliss.

A Pocket Full of God

I am your true desire ... and
I am the goal of liberation too.

So … your direct route to me is not from the exterior but the interior. Therein lies your greatest mystery, and the most beautiful discovery and answer. I am willing you. I am waiting for you. Know yourself and you will know me, as I care and love you… always.

Chapter 4

Divinity

Understand that your Divinity is not measured by the style or size of the home in which you reside, nor the vehicle you drive or even the clothes you wear. One's race, colour or creed bear no relevance or influence either. In addition, your soul or 'higher self' can only be revealed through our connection, and in silence you'll realise this bond cannot be broken by time, space, ether or any other dimension … so it can be said that we are 'united' in love.

It is quite clear and apparent, that to embark upon your own journey of truth (no matter what religion you believe in or faith you follow) your Divinity needs to be re-awakened … removing the mistaken belief in the so-called 'reality' of the physical world.

All you see, hear, touch, taste and smell are

mere reflections of the joy and the eternal wonderment residing within you. Indeed, all the bodily senses—and so much more—are magnified there (way beyond the comprehension and normal thought process of most human beings) because everlasting bliss and peace cannot be found in the denser realm of the physical plane.

✠ ✠ ✠

My love is free—deep inside you—and reflects your own Divinity. Resembling a beacon, it illuminates infinitely beyond the boundaries of your home or wherever else you reside.

By withdrawing from the impermanent world (even for a short while) into stillness and peace, you will become energized and motivated in your well-being. The well of your heart is the only place where you can quench the thirst within your soul. In addition, strength and power will follow through the nourishment of love and truth deep inside you.

✠ ✠ ✠

The permanent 'Atma' known as your Divinity can never fade and die and is as beautiful and majestic as it has always been.

Divinity

People ask, "Who am I?", but this question is just a reflection of what is deemed a secret, and the real desire and goal for all souls. As such, you are me and I am you, the 'I am that I am' or GOD in me 'IS'.

These are two of the countless expressions which try to convey and represent me in words. This is impossible because I am the formless 'form' and the nameless 'name', and only by finding the reality within will you find me to understand the truth.

You can call upon the Angels and Archangels, the Saints and all my light hierarchy (through me), which are at your full disposal. Please believe with all your heart, the same Divinity which lies therein. In this way, no cancer, illness, shadow or pain of darkness and doubt can ever keep us apart. Death of the body is a mirage ... I love you and our oneness is eternal, remember?

Like film inside an old camera, one can stay falsely contained in its casement called the 'body'. The flash (light) of the mind only illuminates when it is ready to, which deceives many into thinking the world is full of shadow and doubt when it is not.

Therefore, the negativity needs to be transformed through this pretend and so-called darkroom of Earth to reveal the picture of truth. Once exposed, the mind and heart and soul (in unison) can bear witness to the glory of our love.

Like a jigsaw puzzle, the pieces of one's life come together, which can then be displayed for all to view who, what and why you truly are Divine.

✠ ✠ ✠

True peace comes to those who do not desire anyone or anything. Those that dilute and dissolve their ego find inner peace more quickly, and subsequently discover their higher self. This brings illumination and recognition of their own Divinity and me. Once you recognise this, understanding new knowledge becomes easier, life is more fulfilling, and you can blossom into the Soul you strive to be.

Divinity

Realise by living in truth, you cannot fear. In dispelling fear, you will know I am near. When you recognise I am near, you will sense my internal voice. Then, when you hear me, knowledge and wisdom enable you to find your true self, a living flame born from a spark, which glows eternal and shines mercifully from our 'one' true heart.

I know you better than you know yourself, for your soul is eternally linked by the bond and connections of love. Hence, the 'records' of who, what and where you have ever been (and experienced) is available to me as the eternal witness to the truth.

Please understand, unlike a 'black-box' within an aircraft, which can become detached (its information and history lost or destroyed over a limited time, or from fire or water) no such occurrence can ever take place with your love and soul.

Everything man-made is impermanent, but Divinity is everlasting, and cannot be misread or misinterpreted in the permanence of the light.

❈ ❈ ❈

Comprehend your heart is my own too, and as an undying flame you are entrusted to shine and illuminate as brightly as you can ... not because I request or would ever demand this, but because you yourself wish to honour and uphold your own spark of Divinity.

This also helps to reveal the right path for those starting their journey, or if they have lost their way, deviating from the pathway of their own truth.

❈ ❈ ❈

Those dividing lines erected through different languages and colours of the skin are false, formed by the illusion and confusion being cast out by those who believe they can manipulate both the body and soul when they cannot.

Remember, throughout history, bodies of many enlightened hearts may have been broken, but the Divine essence and spark of love is immeasurable, unique, and eternal. It cannot be

Divinity

cut down by sword or tongue, burnt, buried, or dissolved; for it is permanent and everlasting.

I can only help you through helping yourselves, not because I won't or can't, but because it's through your own innate Divinity (and the acceptance and understanding of such) which unites all sparks of light into one flame of truth.

Do not be mistaken or believe these last few words appear to divide you, for they do not. As most of the world's population think they are separate and different from each other; I therefore need to highlight and express this in these terms, so you can find the way forward as individuals and together as one body of humanity.

Our connection cannot be severed, and as such our Divinity is my crowning glory for all to witness and partake.

Through infancy, one's youth, in middle or even old age, there is the opportunity to shine utilizing your love, which I have presented and pre-sent to you with all I am.

By opening your heart, all who draw close will recognise the light and share in something precious to behold, for all eternity. This is my timeless gift to all life.

Appreciate you are not a body with a soul but are a soul who wears this denser energy like an overcoat or vessel, which enables 'experience' and emotions to materialise as an expression of me.

However, when you remove the senses (by turning inwards) you will remember the truth of our Universal connection. You could call this a union, a partnership or even a blessing.

The only other way you will rediscover or accept this fact is when the physical is discarded, and the recognition to take place.

Some may find this extremely upsetting and controversial, particularly when a soul undertakes a short sojourn ('soul-journey') into the impermanent world, such as a new-born baby or young child.

With this notion, do not be disturbed, confused, or cry out with anger or frustration, because you are all Divine. As strange as it may seem, karmic choices are made prior to each embodiment.

Divinity

There are still those who choose not to believe in their own Divinity (and therefore in me), preferring to view theories of evolution for example, as the prerequisite to mankind's presence upon the Earth.

I never condemn or belittle such viewpoints but wish you to know … only through an open heart can you attempt to experience the true potential of life and energy beyond the body and mind.

Remember, these both reverberate on a denser and much slower rate of vibration, so they can inhibit and restrict advanced frequencies from piercing through the ether towards your higher self, your consciousness and soul.

Comprehend that I am not hidden away, deep in a forest or a secluded mountain cave. I am not within the ground, buried as a secret treasure, lost for all time. I am not upon the seabed either, drifting back and forth like the currents of the ocean. No, I am inside your heart. Therefore, you hold, nourish, and sustain me too, while keeping me safe … though many do not realise it.

※ ※ ※

Through kindness, joy, truth and love, your Divine essence and spark of true Creation can once more shine like a beacon.

Thus, you become a standard-bearer and torch carried aloft, like an Olympic flame that announces the arrival and coming together of all people as one.

This is not a competition between you, to see who comes 'first', but, by the union of souls, all will stay on the right track.

Appreciate the events of your lives can produce the fields of dreams, encouraging and carrying you forward into eternity.

As I am all things and all things I am, sense and know me in every tree, leaf, rock, blade of grass, flower, the air you breathe, the food and water you consume, the stars, planets, moons, and the Cosmos.

If you can trust me of this, you will trust in yourself. And, if you can believe that I am—and can do what I state—your life will become 'lighter', like floating upon still waters … buoyant, uplifted and sustained forever in my heart.

Divinity

While food and water are the sustenance and fuel of the body, the soul will never be satisfied with bite-sized chunks of nectar, for once you dip your toes, you will want to dive headfirst into your own Divine essence.

This can cause unintentional shockwaves to your family, friends, or acquaintances, as they may view and treat you differently. However, only by living in truth and with courage and conviction (and most importantly with love for each other) can these then be turned into softer ripples and soothing energy.

Realise that your own Divinity requires devotion, like cultivating a flowerbed. If left unkempt and unattended, it is easy for weeds to bind and suffocate the plants and flowers, and likewise, your Divine essence and fragrance will not rise from the plumes and petals of your heart.

Remember, when you are still, boundless energy, peace and bliss envelop your mental, physical, and spiritual/ethereal bodies. By experiencing this (as my love which encompasses you), tears may fall upon your face, but inside the chambers of your heart, they crystallize and shine from your soul, which reflects your effervescence and brilliance like a star. It is here I see your Divine nature revealed, for no secrets can ever lie hidden.

❇ ❇ ❇

I shall never leave you and always love you. Your heart is my own, and your life can be an expression of the Divinity that is you. Be at peace and complete your destiny ... knowing your dreams are my dreams, and I will help you to fulfil them all. We are 'one', always and forever.

❇ ❇ ❇

My Divinity is not discriminatory, because I exist for every living thing. Some say it is often hidden, but clearly this is not so, for love cascades like crystal waterfalls when a nation is grieving, and the people united when loss or tragedy strikes or shakes it to its core.

Such occasions show true strength and bring forth depths of immense courage and character

Divinity

too. Indeed, landscapes and nations across the world are sometimes painfully and comprehensively altered, but during each diversity and challenge you all face, I am holding on to you, and I will never let you go.

Chapter 5

Karma

Karma is action ... played out through memory (accumulated past information) and experience.

Your karma behaves like glue. Further imbalance gets stuck through the adhesive of each transgression of cosmic law—from your thoughts, words, and deeds. Understand that partaking from the font of forgiveness and compassion will help to transmute karma ... for they are the universal solvent, the panacea you require.

Only the layers of sticky black molasses of karma affixed to your life-energy betray and falsify the truth of you. So, unless the individual 'body' removes these through good conduct, right action and with love, then one's true being remains blinded … both consciously and subconsciously until small and more frequent changes are made. That said, by being joyful in every aspect of your life, these so-called yardsticks would bear no relevance whatsoever!

✠ ✠ ✠

Many people think I hide during their perceived tough times in their life, like a thief in the night lurking between the shadows. Please do not feel this way; because your joy reflects in me (and is mine too) … as is the pain of one's body, soul, and mind.

Therefore, everything you experience becomes a record upon the memory. This is inevitably linked by karmic debt from those so-called 'good or bad' deeds generated through love and light and darkness.

✠ ✠ ✠

Remember, I bear witness to everything, including the stillborn child laying in a mother's arms, or the disappearance of a beloved next of kin or pet, seemingly vanished as if into thin air. I sense all pain, emitted like arrows or spears from screaming hearts or those deafened in silence and despair.

Please listen carefully (and try to understand), that in your deepest, darkest hour, you may imagine you disown me, or ask, tell, or shout at me over why I did not help or intervene. Know this query is but a veil, trying to cover love in shadows of doubt and fear, along with anger as a cloak of mystery.

Appreciate your life is a lesson, and an opportunity to express joy. You are experiencing and living because you are 'Creation' in 'action'. You are energy, you are love, all connected like links of an unbroken chain to each other and to me, for we are 'one'.

True strength remains hidden, like underpinning, which carries the weight of wood, brick, or stone. So too with love, for it bears those burdens of your own karmic debt.

However, the walls of faith can rise once more. When built with trust they become even stronger, for it acts in the same way as mortar; interlacing to form an impregnable barrier keeping exterior negativity, trouble, and strife at bay.

Together they give you hope to overcome such things because you will realise the real enemy comes from your own uncertainty and despair.

✠ ✠ ✠

To clear unbalanced karma, simply enter your true heart, for I sit at the seat of every soul. My Divinity is part of the eternal flame of golden love, where magnificent light emanates and permeates in all directions, flowing in a constant gentle stream, washing, and wearing away the rocks of your sin you yourselves created. This will gradually erode (or instantly make it vanish), for purity and truth shine without boundaries, and can conquer all fears and ills.

✠ ✠ ✠

If you release the truth, it pours like water over rock. In time, this will wear down those hardened, karmic imperfections and attitudes … ego, jealousy, pride and not just your own, but in many others too.

In reality, your love may only trickle down at first, resembling a tear falling from your face, but with perseverance, effort and with an appreciation of life, it will shine like the Sun and flow like the ocean, touching every shoreline and heart and blessed with my grace.

※ ※ ※

By clearing your karma, you find balance. When you obtain balance, you discover contentment and peace. Recognizing peace through 'self-realisation', you enter bliss. Once here, you appreciate you are totally free and 'home' … forever besides, within, without, above and below me, you are me.

※ ※ ※

Your duty is to become more responsible for your own thoughts and words and deeds. One can guide or assist another, but inevitably you are your own judge and jury regarding your conduct and pathway in this lifetime. Should you ever think or ask, "Dear God, how am I doing?" The reply you receive resembles the effect following the cause.

※ ※ ※

It is the perception and reaction to every minute of your existence, which helps to determine so much in your lives. Do you see good or evil? Do you trust or mistrust? Do you fear or conquer fear? Do you love or do you allow love to pass you by? Do you give or just take? Do you share ... or even care?

✠ ✠ ✠

The outer 'wrapping' of the body is impermanent and will end up being buried or burnt. Well, I am not concerned with everything that envelopes your Divinity within, for your looks and appearance and material wealth are all unsustainable by-products.

On one's rebirth, you possess nothing of the world that you enter, and subsequently on your return to the source of your identity you are 'without' too. Only the essence and growth of your soul remain intact, and one's karmic memory will have played its part in balancing, erasing or even multiplying this through the experiences of the embodiment.

✠ ✠ ✠

Please try to let love stream from, through and to you. Opportunities will present themselves in every aspect of your existence, and within your home, family, work, and social lives too. Each one can be utilized and shared for truth and honesty, without prejudice and with sincerity.

Karma

They resemble butterflies' wings which silently beat upon the breeze, and yet they carry echoes of peace and kindness to resonate over mountains of ego and pain captured over countless lifetimes.

When the door of truth is ajar, the shaft of light will erase the shadow, forcing it to disappear behind you. At this point you will become a witness to your own reality, which both captivates and frees you from the false burdens and anguish you have made.

Appreciate one should not fear what lies before you in this lifetime but see the path ahead as an opportunity beyond your dreams. Understand that if you cannot agree with this, then you cannot accept yourself or me.

There can be no half measures when you strive for purity. It may seem wise to try to disguise what has been said and done, like brushing dust or rubbish under a carpet, but out of sight will never mean out of mind.

Such things are no different to stored karma, and through those kind or 'Godly' acts, one assumes they bring balance, equilibrium, and order from chaos, but unless 'action' is undertaken with clarity of thought, the outcome is only fleeting. It would be like mowing the grass, which will always need to be re-cut, and the level to which the blades are set bears no relevance at all.

※ ※ ※

Your body is impermanent and dying the moment the physical is 'reborn' … therefore it is important to look after it to help you achieve so much more in your life. In addition, others may call a person's body 'incomplete' … but do not believe you are any less a person (or a being of light and love), within the eyes of my heart.

Realise, everyone is whole to me, and your history and karmic memory has no bearing in whether you deserve to succeed in your true goal or not. Though this is a fact, people can do stupid things for crazy reasons, so each of you is responsible for the choices you make at any point in your life.

Chapter 6

Love and Light

I am love and light, I am all power and all Creation too. Hence it should be easier to realise I am also your breath and heartbeat, and when you feel the way you do, I do too.

Therefore, when you talk, walk, work, rest, or play, express your true feelings so others can share theirs. When your thoughts, words, and deeds are given in truth, every consequence will become mine. Do not worry, for I am within, without, above, below, in front and behind you. As I have stated many times, you are never alone, for I love you with all that I am.

Love is the greatest power of all … for it contains everything. It is light and the dark, hope and fear, freedom or a prison, joy and bliss or pain. Realise love and hate go hand in hand too, so do not try to divide or say this is isn't so, for you will fail.

Deep inside you, this power beckons to be released. Sometimes it trickles to the surface or cascades like fountains and waterfalls from your eyes and heart. When your tears fall in truth, they resonate and glisten resembling dew upon snowdrops in brilliant sunshine. They can sparkle like snowflakes captured by moonlight on a cold frosty night … or sing softly as gentle lullabies to a new-born child. Comprehend and distinguish this as the power and glory, but also the pain.

✠ ✠ ✠

Our love does not hide or pretend to another, because one cannot fake tears of true joy or pain. In moments of immense grief, the mind is oblivious to exterior words, but the heart—torn in two—will become one again. I promise you that this will unclench your fists, and even though you imagine you might succumb to such anguish … I am the glue and the light to mend what you believe is non-repairable.

✠ ✠ ✠

You are all equal, and inside the heart are the same, made from love to expand love. Physical appearances suggest your differences, but it is your own perception of such that separates and causes the divisions within your societies, countries, and the world.

Appreciate too that the core of all life is identical, and in every galaxy and element of light, only the awareness of the truth and level of intellect is different. This, together with a soul's comprehension of its own reality and existence, creates individuality and character, which comes across as being unique and so diverse from each other.

The dialect of many tongues, the colours of one's skin, your gender, shape, and size all show dissimilarities, but love is the energy which unites you all; every creature, being and soul. It is the ultimate power. The universal language of love is boundless and flows from and through and to all 'life'. In fact, it cannot be destroyed by time, distance, or any dimension. As this is so, you are the same too... already immortal inside my heart and forever sustained within my name.

A Pocket Full of God

You may have responsibilities for family, children, and pets and much more besides, but imagine you are casting out a huge net. With the love within you can cast it out far and wide, everywhere you go and everywhere you have been... not just in and around your immediate next of kin.

Therefore, become aware of (and more open to) this reality. Feel the love I send, because we are all one light, one energy ... inseparable.

Always believe in yourself too. I promise you, if you have confidence you will never look back. Do not doubt the love and light inside because my grace presides over every element of life, from the tiniest creature or flower to all beings throughout Creation.

Is it favoured or rationed? No, even though some imagine or believe I do this. And so, please look deep into your heart, because beyond the boundaries of the body and mind you will know me and experience your own truth there too.

✠ ✠ ✠

Realise we are connected by chains of love and light, and those magical cords of truth into eternity. As such, be who you were born to be and do not waste time ... become fulfilled in the

Love and Light

knowledge you are already free.

Illuminate and shine all you are and can be from 'within'. Others will soon remember their own reality too and understand their true 'history' to reveal my gift, which I pre-sent to carry you all ... every day through the future, and throughout the aeons of time.

I often see fractured emotions and many red eyes from falling tears, which leave traces and scars across hearts resembling ploughed fields. But in such weakness, if you can start to trust in me (and yourself) I will make you strong.

Once more, new shoots of opportunity and growth will find their way up and through the fertilized soil (Soul), being blessed by my grace, grown with my love, and sustained by my light.

Remember, by finding and cultivating one's own truth with both passion and integrity, your hopes and dreams will rise and flourish. You will soon untangle yourself ... so you just need to believe.

Sow the seeds of love in the fertile ground of your consciousness. Sprouts of mercy will emerge and assist you, so let the deeds of action and truth multiply far beyond the walls of your home.

The internal and external barriers will fall, enabling more people to bear witness to the real 'you', and realise that love and light is everything. You are all eternal, and I see and know and love you, remember.

Conflict, malnutrition, anger, hate and fear cross over continents around the world like an airborne virus. Only by utilizing the filters of non-discrimination and compassion and also discernment can you make the correct choices and decisions to transfer and dilute such negativity, thus bringing a new calmness to humanity and Mother Earth.

So, where are these golden nuggets of love, light, and truth? Are they stored on supermarket shelves or cast beyond your cost and reach? No, for I am constant, available 24/7, not divided or separated by any religion, faith, colour, creed, or caste. Comprehend I am no 7/11 convenience 'store' either, unavailable through the night or only within certain places, towns, or cities.

Please know that love is the only form of healing which can disperse and eradicate hate. Through loving words and thoughts and actions, the hardened shell of deceit can be broken to reveal the truth in all its glory. In this process, light emerges which can then infiltrate the darkness, creating a clearer direction for all minds and hearts.

Love becomes weak when emotions are enforced, cajoled, or manipulated because it dissipates and remains wafer-thin.

Like ice, any stress or pressure between two hearts can cause it to crack and splinter, creating holes not so easily repaired unless great patience and forgiveness and compassion take hold.

In contrast, unconditional love is understood and felt over great distances, it stays truthful and withstands the test of time, able to travel across and through many dimensions of energy.

Whether you're a mother, father, child, brother, sister, carer, employee, manager, director, orphan, immigrant, politician, or a King or Queen (and so on and so forth), know they simply 'clothes' you were born into, and as such, make no difference to me.

However, you should all act and wear them with justice and fortitude. Know that everyone serves each other in some way, shape or form … and service, help and support to any other life is the only way to display love and kindness too.

Remember, no one can destroy the connection of love between two hearts, even if memory fades or time seems to erase what was once so strong.

In fact, fire, water, earth or sky are unable to cremate, erode, bury, or elevate this bond away, and because it is impossible to extinguish, there is no need to cry, no matter what the circumstances and events seem to conspire or bring to your door.

Love and Light

Our love will burn each false desire, and keep you warm on those days you feel frozen by indecision and uncertainty. It is the one 'fuel' which cannot disappear, unlike the natural resources deep within the Earth consumed by mankind, which will eventually dissipate and be no more.

Understand, it is the most powerful, sustainable energy imaginable. You are unable to buy, bargain for, manipulate, bend, or break it against its will. Love cannot be contained by any other force or dimension and hence is permanent, going beyond the veil of so-called death. It is the greatest gift I give to you, for you to grow, learn and realise you only come full circle... back unto yourself.

In your every endeavour, compassion should always prevail towards your fellow man and the creatures and animals who inhabit the 'Earth-plane' too. Forget all notions of discrimination, because the colour of your skin and the language you speak bears absolutely no relevance in the heart. The beauty of love is without barriers … in any way or shape or form.

A Pocket Full of God

You are free … freedom which is inherent from me. You have the freedom to be whom and what you want in all situations and places, but always determine what you think, say or do are truthful or not.

The ability to be kind, generous and considerate lies inside, which enables you to be a person with true values as a human being—who helps to expand the hand of friendship and love. One can also express these traits through your own creativity too as no walls or bars can contain this asset and the real power of 'you'.

For humanity to thrive and continue to grow in truth, one must display tolerance and forgiveness in equal measure. Try to offer encouragement and kindness, not only beyond the physical expression of materialism but emotionally and mentally too.

One's strength not only encapsulates your embodiment but also represents and brings stamina to your thoughts and fortitude for the heart.

❈ ❈ ❈

Be aware that love is, was and forever shall be. You are never without love, even when you wish to shout or tear your hair out, or if think your head is going to burst open. When this feeling rears its ugly head, simple things can ease difficult problems, for instance, a breath of fresh air, listening to your favourite song, or being with someone or something close to your heart.

Your light is like many burning suns, with both rays and plumes of majestic and colourful energy which spiral in every direction. No earthly structure or any atmospheric pressure, can contain or dampen its true essence from penetrating through distance or time.

Even so, negative thoughts, personified by actions of anger, hate, jealousy and fear will still attempt to hide, disguise, or interrupt the flow of love. Their effects may appear stronger at first, but know they are only short-lived because of the impermanent world where you currently reside.

Dismantle those barriers and obstacles, which are placed in and around your heart. Show the world who and what you are as a true being of light ... a soul who shines and illuminates, bringing happiness and joy to all whom you meet.

Forget now the past, for your own future emerges from this present day in which you walk and talk and act, and by letting each moment bring peace, even into the heart of just one other person, you also help them to accept their own Divinity too.

✠ ✠ ✠

Whether someone's anguish and apparent loss or separation occur through the death of a loved one … true love is eternal. What I speak of is inside you and beyond all transient things.

The passage of time is unable to remove or break it. Distance becomes a false boundary. No one can manufacture this in some worldly place… neither can you buy, sell, deceive, persuade, or cajole unconditional love, because purity is not 'born' and therefore cannot die. It is, was and always will be.

✠ ✠ ✠

What can you say or do when your tears fall? What solution, glue, medicine, or cure do you think you or even the world needs?

You may believe that you desire the status quo or further balance and equilibrium in your

Love and Light

life, but what you really need is peace, compassion and above all, forgiveness.

But how can this happen when someone will not speak? How do you repair what you cannot touch? How can you look into another's soul when your eyes and heart will not even meet? The answers to all these questions begin and end with you.

With arguments, anger is not transferred when you stay calm and replies are given in whispers because the flame of ego cannot be worked up into a frenzy. This gives the one who remains within equanimity the real power and heavenly peace.

The contaminants of hate, frustration and fear are not digested by the mind and therefore further imbalance is not taken on board.

If one still retains doubt, simply try what I describe, when a disagreement (in its various layers and forms) lands upon your door. This is not a game but living with the true rhythmic state and energy of love.

A new day can bring overwhelming joy, emanating love to and from you in a multitude of ways and expressions. Perhaps a kiss with your husband, wife, or partner, or maybe seeing the glory of Creation in the sunrise, or by observing the planets, moon, or stars.

What about sensing raindrops on your skin, the wind in your hair, hugging a family member or friend, or even having your beloved pet by your side?

Indeed, love resonates in truth and truth in love, for it cannot be confined by any being or beast, nor divided or separated between light and darkness or erased by time and distance.

Only your self-doubt and confusion can lead you away from me, further than what you think or believe you now are. No, I am nearer than near, like the blood running through your veins and the conscience which pricks your mind, after one's thoughts, words and deeds have materialised.

You are all entwined and connected, resembling threads woven together to form the truth ... but

Love and Light

without the structure of life-energy (and love), you would cease to exist as soul, body and mind.

In fact, like a jumper without a hole for your head, a necklace with a missing link, or a plane with only one wing, nothing would function and be a worthwhile expression of Creation.

Understand too, that the colour of your skin, your shape/size (or even if you imagine you are incomplete in some way) make no difference because you are forever 'whole' and Divine.

Expand your light beyond the walls where you live or work so friendships may form. Nations of people can then blossom as one body to exude the fragrance of love and peace across the world ... cast upon my breath.

The nectar of my being will flourish on fertile soil and within all hearts. Tears of joy and rays of hope from the Sun will nourish and sustain those who partake in truth. Weeds of deceit, hate, anguish and pain shall be removed through your determination, perseverance, and faith.

Each of you are living, burning, flames of light. Indeed, every soul forms the plumes of my heart, and together we are whole.

So, whether you are residing in a mansion or palace, in a slum or even a tent, these material surroundings are impermanent and transitional. Only when you realise you are forever surrounded by my love and grace, will the permanence of truth be retained, and eternally rest inside your heart.

※ ※ ※

By cultivating the roots of love through right action, many souls and minds can grow stronger, withstanding any winters of discontent to rise into the Sun. The individual and the masses are not then suffocated by despair, anxiety, and stress, which attempt to strangle the purity of truth which flows from above and below.

If you can tend to the 'garden' of virtues each day, those weeds of doubt, frustration and fear will be eradicated over time. Similarly, through your own efforts to plant seeds of compassion, right-conduct, and peace, they will all flourish through the nurturing of one's heart.

So, by acknowledging and letting these reign inside you, your life will bloom and become more colourful. And, like a photograph, it will remain as a permanent reminder of your efforts, captured within a lens of light.

✠ ✠ ✠

Do you think I can make mistakes? If the answer is no, why do you worry, become anxious, or cast thoughtful doubts into the ether? With so many miracles around you, where can the illusion and confusion come from? Can you not see or sense nature from and through the window? Are love and light and truth not constantly displayed for every one of you to survey?

✠ ✠ ✠

Try to appreciate, I am the songs from those birds who communicate with each other. I am the owl, crow, fox and all elements of life which call to their young, in the hope to teach, guide and support them until they are ready to understand how to live … and become 'detached'.

✠ ✠ ✠

Do not fear when I am near—and try to be grateful for all that you are, all that you have, and all that you can become.

✠ ✠ ✠

Thoughts of a single person can help to change the many. Therefore, by tending one's own garden (your character and personality) to live and nurture true human values, the seeds of love will sprout further afield.

You could picture vast acres of barren soil and weeds, but through perseverance and understanding of your fellow man's needs, they become full of light and spiritual growth. Like a patchwork quilt, they can be sewn together to form a collective layer of hope and peace, covering the world in a blanket of love.

When all souls acknowledge that the same God/Creator residing inside them also lives in the heart of another, love and light shall cascade like fountains in all directions.

Do not ever doubt this but continue to unite beneath the banner of your hearts, so that the people of the world can hear, see, and help those overcome pain and disharmony, bringing relief for one and all.

One day, humanity's anguish will fade, as hopes and dreams become fulfilled with sincerity and peace into eternity.

✵ ✵ ✵

Unlike a ripple upon calm waters, love's action transmutes way beyond the pebble thrown into the pool of life, so understand there are no boundaries which cannot be broken or erased.

Differences in colour, creed or religion are on the surface, and 'man' needs to dig deep to discover the truest connection of all.

✵ ✵ ✵

If just one person strives to change his character and life while sharing from the fountain of truth within, my love and light will pour from the well of their heart. Many will come to drink the goodness drawn forth and thereby quench thirst so parched. Your Divinity and essence will shine across the Earth and throughout the world's community, and then you can all become the true beacons of joy and hope everlasting.

✵ ✵ ✵

Remember, the sun will always rise somewhere upon the Earth-plane. Likewise, love always rises to the surface of your heart when you let your smile, handshake and every thought, word and deed be the reflection from oneself ... to simply 'self'. Try, therefore, to believe the chill of discontent (or negative times) is a mirage and may each morn' bring a warm glow to radiate through your kindness and laughter forever and a day. In doing so, you will discover your true power, and ultimately find me.

Humanity and nature must begin to live more in harmony. Harnessing the assets and beautiful energy from the planet you reside upon (in positive ways), would be a start.

Man needs to comprehend all life is sacred because each animal, insect and creature contains my love and truth.

The only difference between these and yourselves is the fact the kingdom of nature does not know it (yet). They are not 'God' conscious or aware, man is.

Every one of you can lead by example, but not for plaudits or to satisfy or stroke the ego, because truly helping each other is as inherent within you as your own DNA.

To ignore the plight or pain of any other form of life is not a chromosome deficiency or so-called birth 'defect' or disability.

No, those decisions are from an ill-conceived character and personality; selfish, unloving and in denial of one's true purpose and goal.

Acts of kindness, when carried out with love, reverberate throughout time, and leave an imprint on hearts and souls. These do not fade like footprints on wet sand, or handprints cast as reminders in clay or cement, as they will all disappear ... even if this takes thousands or millions of years, because this is inevitable on the impermanent world.

Each substance in creation has its vibration, its own 'keynote'. As such, in all sacred texts and 'written word' throughout time, every consonant, vowel, phrase, sentence, paragraph and book resonate at their own frequency.

Because of this, their understanding remains fixed, resembling deep-rooted trees, or they float like feathers and leaves upon the breeze.

Therefore, if your vibrational state/life-energy matches the energy of what is read or heard, the information, knowledge and wisdom become easier to digest, as the recognition of truth falls into place.

Over time, the love which flows to, through and from you (in conjunction with your own efforts) will shine forth like a flower bud opening on a warm sunny day.

Within you, the plumes of your eternal fire will glisten and sparkle like open petals caught by a shower of rain in the hot summer sun. Your magnificence is then displayed forevermore, as you finally understand that your own brilliance is without limitation.

Remember, I do not favour rich or poor, tall or small, fat or thin, so let the colours of truth, love and light be the pallet of one's heart, which brings your own soul's picture to life.

Love and Light

I urge you to ignore all fear which only binds you. Comprehend you are 'love' ... to love, by love, in love and through love. If you deny this you are also denying me ... but if you accept your true self, you are accepting me with all your heart and soul and mind and in all things too. In fact, this is the simplest explanation of them all.

✠ ✠ ✠

I love you all. If you can love your true self, in turn, you will love all life and so the world can change for the better. Indeed, the rising of emotional waters will subside, and anger will dissipate. Eruptions shall disappear, and those clouds of toxic and violent 'energy' will no longer threaten but disperse, leaving a much cleaner, purer atmosphere for all to live and breathe. Believe it, and it will be so.

✠ ✠ ✠

Remember, as long as you face the Light, the shadows are always behind.

Chapter 7

Health and Wealth

You often hear that 'true wealth is your health', and therefore it is important to understand that if you are healthy you have an advantage (and the ability) to conquer those worldly desires with greater ease.

A lack of joy and contentment in life will also hinder or prevent you from knowing the truth of what, why and who you 'are'.

❈ ❈ ❈

The 'material' aspect of living (and especially money) may influence the opinions of many people or indeed the whole world in what they think of you, but this can never disguise the inner 'you' from me.

Appearances count for nothing in love and truth, for it is your true character and personality that depicts the light emanating from your soul.

Sadly, people will often imagine something is missing in their lives, but they do not know or realise what this could be. Comprehend that real peace and contentment will never be found in a new car or home or anything else made upon the impermanent plane.

A chink of light exists though, for if you listen to the one voice of truth (inside the stillness which beckons), you can start to believe there is so much more to your current situation and life. Bliss of the boundless awaits.

✠ ✠ ✠

You are loved in all situations, whether one is in poverty or rich beyond their wildest dreams … though only those who live in these respective scenarios can say if they are joyful and content.

Monetary riches cannot buy you love and peace and never will. It can make you feel more comfortable and may give you the ability to make choices of where you can live, but money will never show you how to live.

✠ ✠ ✠

You must accept your looks will fade, that hair turns to grey, the skin will crinkle, and no amount of makeup can hide the truth of age.

Health and Wealth

From the moment of your birth the clock is ticking, and the countdown to death of your physical body had begun. One's birthday or New Year celebrations have (unfortunately) become the forgotten annual reminders of your own mortality.

However, through knowing your true self, you can achieve a great deal, simply by accepting and sharing much joy in your life.

※ ※ ※

Time should not be squandered on being something you are not, or by trying to portray a picture of someone who you think others wish to see. Be you … it is enough.

※ ※ ※

Hatred can ooze from every cell of the body and must be erased. Know that hate brings anguish, anguish leads to fear, fear leads to stress, and stress is 'disease' (ill at ease … dis-ease) and ultimately, brings death to the body.

It also represents the blindness to another's love and joy, and like a reflection within a strange mirror at a funfair, it distorts and contorts the true image of life and light itself. In addition, hatred leads you away from the rays of the Sun (and Son), which beam with such radiance both inside and out.

The ugliest mask of all is deceit because even if looked upon with rose-tinted glasses, the 'truth will always out'. There are no secrets which can be kept from me. And, should you believe the hands of time will make things fade or hide—by being buried under layers of illusion—when one dies, it still remains.

False pleasure and attachments resemble a stone tossed into a clear pool of water, causing concentric rings to ripple outwards. At first, they are seen very clearly, but will soon fade and disappear … as if they never happened at all. This signifies the weight of a fictitious hope, which sinks into the depths of your memory and attempts to cling to your heart through your emotions.

Do not be concerned over what the exterior garment reveals, but appreciate it is the inner 'I' which illuminates and transcends. In fact, your character and personality and above all your heart (rather than the bodily appearance and

Health and Wealth

image that is portrayed), will always shine in truth by what is said, and more importantly, done.

You may create as many illusions as you wish to make. You can even try to deceive yourself from being who you are, but light sees all as an eternal observer to reality. Indeed, people often attempt to deny others from viewing their true selves, but I bear witness to your entirety.

Only anxiety or dread of something (or someone) will cause such a need, but like I always say, do not fear when I am near.

You may create as many illusions as you wish to make. You can even try to deceive yourself from being who you are, but light sees all as an eternal observer to reality. Indeed, people often attempt to deny others from viewing their true selves, but I bear witness to your entirety.

Try living in the present and be joyful and content, then concerns of the past and fears for the future will disappear. This is not a course or route where if one fails to plan you plan to fail, quite the opposite!

When you regain control of your thoughts, words and deeds then 'right' action prevail, and only goodness ensues (in terms of what is seen and felt or heard) … not only for yourself but of those around you too.

In addition, please do not succumb to negativity, as this rips holes into the fabric of your well-being ... it picks away at your positive thinking and can cause irreparable damage to your self-confidence.

Instead, trust that I am the 'I' (eye) of the needle, which is your first defence, mending tirelessly with you, together as one. So, you see, there are many similarities between the clothes of the body and the cloth of your soul. Ultimately, it is always your own choice to establish if one is more than, or equally important as, the other.

Your true wealth is in your personality and character. No one will remember you for how much money you earned or spent, but numerous hearts will have eternal memories of your kindness, compassion and forgiveness as your soul makes its way through karma and time.

Chapter 8

Religion and Belief … Faith and Trust

No matter where you live or country you were born, all are 'one'. Religion or belief should not dissipate this notion, for the foundation and basis of all should be love. So, whether you are a Christian, Muslim, Hindu, Sheik or of any nationality, colour, creed, or faith … do not feel or think you are above or below or more or less worthy than another. The seas of the world have different names, but in reality, they are but one ocean.

Many envisage a 'God' who presides over them or a deity who lives in a 'special' place. They may even gaze upon a statue or alter which attempts to depict what I am … but if there is no separation, I am all things.

Remember, I am a wilting flower and the next one to bloom. I am the tree without leaves and the blossom that flies on the wind. I am the desert and the sea's and I am the 'above and below'.

※ ※ ※

It does not make any difference in the religion you follow, nor that I am called 'God' … Creator… or any other name. What is important is that the individual can perceive and identify our all-pervading 'oneness'.

Know that the very essence and life-energy itself have been shared in all its many forms and appearances for growth and learning in every aspect of Creation.

※ ※ ※

Comprehend too, that over many thousands of years my Divinity had to descend upon the Earth-plane in human form … to impart knowledge and wisdom to all those who would listen and open their hearts through faith and trust and to seek the realisation of our oneness.

Mohammad, Jesus, Buddha, Shiva and Krishna (to name a few) were all noted as 'prophets', expressing love and Divine guidance to release you from the bondage of incarnations

Religion and Belief... Faith and Trust

in the gross/denser elements of an embodiment.

Now, the technology of the modern age connects you all around the globe, so there has never been a better time for you to learn and experience and know the truth of you.

✻ ✻ ✻

Christ explained, "I am the bread of life. He who cometh to me shall never hunger, and he who believeth on me shall never thirst".

Appreciate that much guidance was conveyed throughout the ages, but please understand, even if you read sacred texts such as the Bible, the Koran (Qur'an) or the Vedas etcetera, the wisdom that belongs to you and you alone lies in the stillness and Divine nature of your heart.

Like your favourite chocolate or candy, after you taste the sweetness of your own being, you will desire more and wish to share it too.

✻ ✻ ✻

Do not be influenced or led astray by any other person in the world. You can, of course, read any book and visit (or connect with) any sage, scholar, or guru but your own truth will never be theirs and vice versa.

In fact, no one should feel pressured into

another's beliefs, because you are a holder of reality inside your own heart. It is a sacrifice, which needs endeavour to understand, believe and grow through experience. Embracing the love and our connection inside is the only way, as it will lead you straight to me.

※ ※ ※

During difficult times, you should remain courageous in your internal belief system. Do not be overly pessimistic or optimistic but become a realist. Treat everything that occurs with equanimity and this will bring balance to your life. No matter what your colour, race or nationality and religion... kindness and peace and goodwill and compassion all need to prevail.

※ ※ ※

Through trust you live without fear, so do not be concerned or box yourself in with worries or doubts. These will only slow you down, preventing you from picking up pace towards self-realisation. It is enough, therefore, to simply just 'be'.

Remember, do not pretend to be someone who you are not and never feel that you must

Religion and Belief... Faith and Trust

justify your existence to anyone or anything … in any place or dimension. You are who and what you are, and everything around you remain temporary. Forgetting this stems from the mind's illusion … so try to be 'dis'-illusioned!

✠ ✠ ✠

How can you obtain additional protection when troubled times come? Well, one ought to appreciate one's faith can be your umbrella; a shield not only against another's thoughts and feelings, which would like to penetrate your whole being … but also stops you wanting to do the same.

Understand your trust in yourself and me will ensure the overcoat (the body) will function properly. This will insulate you against 'bitter' enemies from within ... and when the intensity of worldly desires whips up and whirl into a frenzied chill of discontent. Later, your own life-energy will enable you to acknowledge the truth of why you must succeed and accept who and what you truly can come to be.

Remember to have strength and conviction in your faith too, with a renewed hope in everything you do. Understand that an increase in confidence of your own ability (to overcome hardship and transgressions) will soon materialize.

✠ ✠ ✠

You may decide to kneel and look up to the 'Heavens' and pray, but unless prayers materialise from deep inside you, the energy and vibration you send are without structure or precision.

But, if your heart is true, the signature of your soul (in its rhythmic state), is heard across time and space and each dimension. There will be no barriers or obstacles, nothing to be concerned or worried about, nor defy or conquer, because I am here and both near and far, and of course, deep inside you too.

✠ ✠ ✠

Please understand, I do not judge such elements of who is right and who is wrong, because the principles and guidelines of human beings are the same. If someone is an atheist, they can still be a so-called 'good' human being!

Likewise, to be a Christian or Muslim or to live by any religious doctrine… is to be true in thought, word, and your deeds too.

Religion and Belief... Faith and Trust

Prayers are the vibrations of love streaming through the ether. In contrast, your body—which contains the energy of our Divine nature—is the source to carry out the process itself, with acts of kindness, support, and empathy. Reflect upon this for a moment, and establish the existence deep inside, as it beholds you all.

Remove all doubt in your abilities, because you are strong, motivated, and full of purpose and direction. If you imagine you are weak ... believe me, you are not.

One's true potency can never lie in the physical stature of the body, for it is revealed only through (and by) passion, creativity, and the truth from inside your heart and soul.

Chapter 9

Body, Mind and Soul

You are all free to choose who and what you can become. Nothing could alter this. So, search within yourself and find the 'Heaven' you seek, because inside your heart is where paradise and unconditional love exists and emanates. So, live in me to find me, and all heartache, problems and stresses will disappear from a troubled mind.

Realise the body is a mask, hiding the truth of what lies beneath/within. Only when your true abilities as a soul begin to shine, can the 'exterior' peel away to reveal one's beauty and peace and as such, becomes easier to recognise your own Divinity.

However, do not consider your own body as ugly, misshapen, somehow incorrect, or even hopeless, as it is both precious and required. Appreciate your shell/overcoat enables you to achieve what you were 're-born' to do and be.

I urge you, therefore, to protect, cherish and fully understand this so-called casing of your soul, but I will never criticise how you live your life, as those decisions are yours, and yours alone to make.

✥ ✥ ✥

Please, do not mistake the physical body as a representation of me, for you were not 'created' in my image this way. Clouds of illusion may try to deceive, but you can blow these away with one breath of hope and faith and love.

I encourage you to bask in the knowledge your soul and heart cannot die or fade to grey, for you are 'life' more colourful than crystals and rainbows, and more beautiful than your mind can ever imagine.

✥ ✥ ✥

Appreciate the light is your essence and fortress, and love is all things, the eternal glue which binds you all to me and me to you. It is permanent and can never descend into ruin.

Remember, only what appears in the impermanent world (where your body resides), can it seem this way.

Body, Mind and Soul

Once humanity realises the oneness of Creation, all the false defences around nation to nation, city to city and those between every person will fall, and these will be the only ruins to be 'celebrated' forever and a day.

✠ ✠ ✠

The body, mind and soul are connected to enable you to grow and experience whilst you reside and resonate on the vibration (sound/energy) of the Earth-Plane.

That said, you are Divine and not bound or restricted in any way at all ... otherwise your love and light would not shine through, from, and to me.

Similarly, how would you dream, or one's intellect, thoughts and feelings float upon the ether to touch one another across time, space, and many dimensions?

✠ ✠ ✠

Whether you are awake or asleep, you are all but a reflection of me. In thought and word and deed and in body and mind and soul, there is no separation or division.

This provides you with the ability to focus on every positive aspect of living and being. It is a choice and so-called 'free will' which therefore dissipates, dilutes, and filters good actions from bad, and the effect from the cause.

Sceptics will say happiness is a state of mind, yet I explain your true contentment lies outside of your mind. Without it, you do not need to conjure up images or control feelings of desire.

People can relate to the words, "I want happiness" or "I want peace", but if you take away the 'I' (which relates to your ego), and take away the 'want' (the desire); you are left with the goal and the truth… peace.

Do not believe you are trapped by fate or by the timing of your 'sojourn' upon the Earth-plane. Remember, your will, energy and creative essence of your Divinity can only be shackled by your own limitations!

For example, even those in physical, mental, emotional, or spiritual pain overcome and achieve wonderful and everlasting moments of beauty and glory.

In fact, they take life with encouragement, perseverance, fortitude, and determination, which transcends both body and mind. These are lasting legacies, captured by memories of love through the heart into eternity.

Please try to rise above any negativity that picks and irritates you physically and psychologically, most of which can be deflected and dissipated by sending out thoughts of peace and kindness.

In time, you can control and change your state of mind as soon as it tries to trick and behold you, then you will become 'lighter' in all your think, say, and do.

Simplicity is the answer during times when doubt or angst raise their ugly head. Simple 'truths' will also provide clarity and enable you to power ahead.

When darkness or gloom descends, please bring light into your thinking. Let the anxiety, fear, and anguish of what has not yet come to pass fade from your brow. Spiritual poise will counter this poison and will guide you from desire, confusion, and illusion both inside and out.

A Pocket Full of God

Remember, one's mind should not dictate to the heart, but it will try to impose its will through your senses, nonetheless. Therefore, the key is balance, and by making it less reactive to your feelings, you become aware of your soul in the important areas of your life.

You are what you are, so whether you are short, fat, tall or thin … these different traits and characteristics do not make you closer or any further away from my heart.

In addition, being black, white, yellow, or red does not make one more loving or more prone to the ugliness of a fight. Anger, hate, jealousy and ego and many other 'negative' elements of the 'self' are not dependent upon such things.

By removing any rose-coloured glasses, you can see with the internal lens of the heart that allows you to witness the truth.

You will understand you are not merely the body, but a soul residing inside a 'vessel' … which enables you to remain in this denser

Body, Mind and Soul

vibration to relearn and grow.

So, with karma removed, collected, or fulfilled, your life shall become 'complete'—be it for only one second or minute, an hour or a day, a month, or a year, or even three scores and ten. The Soul then departs this vessel, which becomes lifeless to the naked eye.

The mind always attempts to reason and justify everything, and this, in turn, grounds your soul with an imaginary ball and chain.

In effect, one is anchored to (and angered with) the physical, joined by frustration and despair. Each becomes a repetitive 'link' in the desire to make the unknown, known.

In comparison, when you let go of preconceived ideas on exactly how to experience the beauty within the realms of Creation, the differences are quite clear.

In times of struggle, pleas and cries and screams ring out piercing me like a dagger. Of course, this is an expression of speech only, for I am beyond all such things.

Nonetheless, emotions become magnified

tenfold when true pain or joy flows from the mind, body, or soul. It is vital, therefore, to filter false anxiety, especially concerning the loss of any material possessions or anything else in the impermanent world.

The eyes often see the worst of things. Your ears may hear Chinese whispers. The tongue frequently speaks untruths. Your hands try to influence or bend 'life' to a false will, and instead of the sweet scent of love … the atmosphere can be drenched with fear from your yesterdays, and the future too.

Sometimes you might imagine your heart is breaking into two, but I am the source who heals and mends, and my light and energy is a magical 'glue'. Then, when your joy and laughter is strong and loud, the echo of such happiness I will send beyond those earthly clouds of doubt.

All I ask is every minute, hour, day, week, month, or year of your life, that your heart opens wider to know my voice deep within, as it reflects the truth inside your soul.

Body, Mind and Soul

Within every life, I constantly leave you clues and messages. Some are subliminal, while others glare you right in your face, and yet they can still be missed!

I might send you the perfect song over the radio, or you could overhear a conversation which triggers a memory or feeling. What about a fragrance too, which reminds you of someone or something personal? Perhaps you will gaze upon a beautiful sunset or bear witness to an incredible picture or photograph? Or … a moment of intimacy creates both joy and comfort deep inside you.

These are but a few examples of how I connect with your own Divine spark, because with this connection, not only do you start to imagine you are 'complete', you become inspired to think about and search for answers in your soul.

Do not despair in striving to establish a meaning of it all. The reality is not in faraway lands to which you cannot reach or find.

Nor is it withheld through the aeons of time by sacred texts or words, which can no longer be deciphered.

There is no secret 'secret', as love is the only

answer. It is the key, the door, the way, and the truth … nothing more and nothing less. If this were not so, you would not even exist.

One day, when you are ready, you'll cast off the dense overcoat of the body, so please do not keep any regrets, and make sure your obituary leaves a legacy and reads true, and becomes an example for others to follow.

When all is said and done, I will lift you upon golden chariots of light, and your Divinity will burn more brightly than a thousand suns. It will radiate in all directions, signalling your arrival, the return and recognition of your real state of being. You will receive a welcome like no other, surrounded by all the love you could ever imagine and more.

Comprehend this is the essence of everything you emit from your heart centre, be it to family, friends, and pets throughout Creation, and this all comes back to you, from every source you recognise and know in truth.

Tears of joy will finally erase the false agony of separation, and at this moment, you will undeniably experience the existence of our unity.

Body, Mind and Soul

I implore all beings and every 'life', please do not let those cries of pain (or so-called injustices) ever tarnish our reality, because not one soul shall pass me by.

In addition, not a single tear will fade or disappear, for they are precious, and I, therefore, catch them all. As I always state, they hang in suspension around me, linked by cords of light, reminding, helping, nurturing you all both inside and out.

They too, shine eternal, like diamonds and stars, which magnify right from wrong, love from hate, peace from war, and the truth illuminates from the biggest lie of all, that death of the body is the 'end'.

Chapter 10

Your Physical and Non-Physical Journey

The important time for you is right now, today ... because tomorrow will take care of itself.

Something will always need doing in your life, with places to be and people to meet ,but please find time to contemplate and become 'still'.

Do not worry about the past, your yesterday. Be aware not to be driven too much by the future either. All that matters are the 'now', the present ... pre-sent to you, and this gift of 'time' (and what you do within the moment) is more precious than you can know.

A Pocket Full of God

I know you have so much to give of yourself ... tremendous joy and hope and energy and light, so please open your heart and do not hide.

Push aside the false notions and ill feelings of doubt and despair which the material world tries to impose upon you. Rise above such things in the knowledge that love always provides you with exactly what you need on your journey.

So, as the days, weeks, months, and years go by, seemingly faster as you age, do you continue as you are (some may say aimlessly), or do you actively pursue the goal in sight?

Will you let your future drift by and fade like a New Year's resolution, or can you identify the power of change within you? Indeed, everyone has a choice; and you only need to decide what to do with the time and the life you have chosen and been given.

Of course, the clock can never be turned back, but each moment in truth shines eternal and can bring you closer to the person and soul inside which you long to be.

Your Physical and Non-Physical Journey

You can help to eradicate negativity and karmic memory that clings or covers the soil (and soul) by being thorough and meticulous with the seeds you sow. Only by sharing peace, love, and kindness will this spread ... covering the ground and path you walk upon, ensuring only goodness will flourish.

Sometimes this may seem difficult, but many hands make 'light' work, and just like a magnet, you will attract or be drawn to like-minded people, and other light-hearted Souls.

✠ ✠ ✠

Spend time contemplating how best to live, sharing the goodwill of your heart on your road to bliss. In thought or prayer do not ask me how far you have travelled or how much further you need to go but continue to gain confidence in the knowledge that I am with you every step of the way.

✠ ✠ ✠

Feel the life-energy and canopy of love which I send to enlighten you all. Likewise, with each new dawn, the warmth of the sun radiates over the land which brings life with a guiding hand, just as the growth of a seed or blade of grass

A Pocket Full of God

grows in the earnest of the light.

When the clouds open to rain down upon the Earth, the world drinks its life-force which maintains its survival. These are simple things that man seems to have forgotten ... how everything connects to sustain and give life.

✠ ✠ ✠

You are living in a world of wonder and beauty, if you are uncertain of this, try to recall your memories of these miracles …

An embrace from a long-forgotten friend, your partner, spouse or with a beloved pet.

Your first kiss.
Love.
Mother nature.
A flower.
Trees.
A sunset or sunrise.
The stars sparkling on a clear night sky.
The glow of a full moon.
A snowflake.
The Sun.
Rain.
A brilliant rainbow.
The air you breath.
Food and water.

Your Physical and Non-Physical Journey

What other experiences are etched deep within the mind, and can now shine from your soul?

※ ※ ※

In the depths of winter and spells of frost, one's environment can appear dull and withered, so it is prudent to view through different lenses.

Unlike those three-dimensional (3D) glasses which attempt to imitate real-life upon a television (tell-lie-vision) screen, please look and experience through your heart instead, as this brings new and pleasant surprises each day.

For instance, birds still fly and sing, while a tree without leaves draws one to the beauty of its bark. Also, when conditions are exactly right, a full moon in the coldness of night will cause the rooftops to shimmer and shine like mirrors, while hedgerows and verges sparkle like stardust, as car headlights compete with nature's rays of light. So, whatever the season, bear witness to all the surrounding miracles.

※ ※ ※

Human beings are not above or below one another. So, who reflects the truth, a blind beggar, or the rich man? Ask yourself too, who has the real vision, those that rise above their senses or use their sight alone?

Be aware that many people close their eyes to their true selves (and what they can become) ... but turn back the pages of history and you will find those who displayed their Divinity and overcome negativity, fear and hate.

So, it is never too late to discover your reality and fill your days with love and joy, which is the challenge for each heart.

People often assume they are participating in a worthless job, or by working in dirty or difficult conditions they are somehow less important than those who appear to be at the top of the 'tree', but this makes no difference to me.

You must, therefore, appreciate your own self-worth because as a soul and heart of light, you are precious beyond compare. I love you, so please accept that those imagined obstacles and tasks to overcome help you develop your character, personality, and should make you stronger too.

Your Physical and Non-Physical Journey

Limitations in your life are made by your own thoughts and words and deeds ... not by my intervening hand. I do not inflict pain or hardship or by making you feel less worthy, unloved, or alone.

Truth is reality ... revealed as waves and beams of light and sound (vibration/energy) and these cannot be manipulated or disguised, like throwing a wet blanket over flames, snuffing out a candle, or by flicking a switch to off.

❈ ❈ ❈

I hope you try to be yourself, and happy in your own skin, and through thick and thin hold onto your own beliefs and faith—if they are true.

Be able to look in the mirror and accept and like what you see. Let everything you think, say, and do also be the real reflection of your own heart, and not what someone else thinks what they wish to see ... or for you to be.

❈ ❈ ❈

I understand that whatever social media, television, radio, or newspapers portray (be it hatred, anger, disease or war), it can be easy to despair and utter words of anguish or sorrow for people, animals and even nature itself.

However, this is precisely when you must realise there is always hope.

※ ※ ※

With times of uncertainty, in what appears an unforgiving world, change your mindset and believe in the goodness and truth which lies within you and in all things.

Reach for it and share this with positive thoughts and prayers for those in need. More importantly, let your hands do the work of love ... to aid, support and guide those who are less fortunate. Remember, hands that 'do' are holier than lips that pray.

※ ※ ※

We breathe and exist as one, and hence I feel what you feel, see what you see, and ride the peaks and troughs of your so-called good and bad times too.

Continue to trust in yourself and me, as your dream of everlasting peace is but a heartbeat away. This is not hidden by me (as if I keep an imaginary door that lies beyond your hopes and dreams), so just keep in mind, there is no lock and key and one's heart is the pathway into eternity.

Your Physical and Non-Physical Journey

When you recognise and appreciate and grow through your life experiences you gain wisdom. This enables you to know and accept you are one with me. If this were not the case, then why do you exist, and what would your true being and purpose be?

If ugliness rears its head, darkness and negativity can start to pick and stab at your consciousness, so how should you react? What can you say or do? This may sound complicated, but it is not. By living truthfully, life is simplicity itself, and therefore, the only answer is love. Through love flows compassion, and vice versa, remember?

Your real character resides in what you say and think and do because they all reflect and resonate love—or lack of. Common phrases like, "So you sow, so shall you reap" and, "What goes around comes around" ring true. I am not asking you to be a Saint, but request you take control of your life and become 'realised'.

Become conscious of all your actions. Do not waste time or money on the impermanent aspects of living either. In the process, dismiss desire and want and greed which do not reflect your true intellect … they will only slow you down in your pursuit of righteousness, liberation, and the glory of your Divinity.

However, you ought to take pleasure in your life because you are 'alive' … and all things, whether they are experienced physically, mentally, emotionally or spiritually (if they do not hurt yourself, or any other form of life), should be enjoyed!

By having confidence in yourself, you retain the same quality in me, and everything becomes easier to bear as I will carry you.

In this knowledge, please put effort into being the best person and human being you can be and try to follow and speak and enact the truth as we have discussed all along.

Your Physical and Non-Physical Journey

Wherever you go, you may appear to be small, insignificant, or even dispensable, but you are not. Like an ingredient missing from a meal, it would not go unnoticed. If you take a single cog from an old clock, its hands will fail to turn. Likewise, a torch would fade and disappear without all the battery cells within it.

Comprehend, there is no difference with each soul … which is why the Earth and humanity need everyone to connect and illuminate in these current times. Can you help one another, and in doing so aid yourself? Will you link in unison, or be as negative and positive, seemingly poles apart?

The ability to rise above so-called bad situations (and circumstances which attempt to drag you under the mire of illusion) resides inside you. Therefore, you have the choice to perceive each new day as further tests to work through, or unique opportunities to demonstrate the latent gifts bestowed upon and within all human beings.

You can control how you feel and react to any given scenario. Only by constantly monitoring your thoughts can you possibly hope to change your emotional, physical, mental, and spiritual energies, both inside and out.

You will then attract the right conditions to bring goodwill, kindness, generosity, and peace into your life, and to the door of your home.

※ ※ ※

Smile when you awake… for you are alive.
Smile every hour.
Smile in adversity.
Smile when you feel joyful.
Smile before you sleep...
And watch your life change for the better!

※ ※ ※

Understand, whether you are knee-deep in rubbish and living life in the 'gutter', or if your body lies upon silk sheets and your head appears to live amongst the stars, appreciate this is all temporary ... fleeting ... transitory.

Only your heart and soul contain the humility to conquer the smugness of false power and ego, or those unwanted depths and lows of what

Your Physical and Non-Physical Journey

seems an unworthiness of self, carried towards your fellow 'man'.

True service must, therefore, start with love, not for self-gain or in pity either, but because it will enable you to elevate the oneness of you all, now and forevermore.

❈ ❈ ❈

Each moment of life provides a possibility to gain and share knowledge and wisdom through one's experiences. If you can simply be glad and not sad, you will see that the peaks and troughs and those ups and downs on your journey ahead can all be enjoyed. Why should you fear the horizon when I am within, beside above and below you?

❈ ❈ ❈

Unlike a chameleon who can blend in with its surroundings, for you to try to disguise one's thoughts, words, or actions from me is pointless, a waste of your precious time, energy, and love.

Please realise though, I am not the camera who spies like 'big brother', but am the 'I' of truth inside, outside, above, below, in front and behind you too. I am your conscience, your intuition and the petals and plumes of your radiating heart which bloom with perfume and fragrance of our love as one.

One must understand, practice does not necessarily make perfect, and to enforce or place pressure of any kind can prove harmful, especially to the young. This is not the same as encouragement, discipline, or endeavour, which are all traits one can either accept or not.

For instance, a mother or father who wishes to see their offspring rise to the top of a profession (or skill) is fine, but that future is not guaranteed. A child's desire for success may not always match (or exceed) their own, so it is essential not to view or live life through other human beings.

Think about the tasks you have completed today. Did they burden you emotionally, mentally, or spiritually? Could you have spoken or acted in a gentler or kind way? Were your thoughts selfless … emerging from the truth, or selfish by design? Was there an occasion to help those less fortunate than yourself? Have you been joyful or miserable? I am only asking.

Can you say there is no room for improvement in your life? If you had nothing to learn, nothing else to do or experience, and if no 'joy' was to come from your presence on the Earth ... then why are you there?

You should dispense with the idea of trying to get through life devoid of challenges because confidence grows when you embark upon the richness of change.

Your life is your making and can be as beautiful and as glorious as you wish to make it ... no matter where you live or in what skin you are born. By living with (and through) good conduct, peace, love, joy, and truth, then each day can glow and become amazingly colourful ... so create!

Throughout childhood and adolescence, you are learning and growing on many levels, and through your experiences, one's actions and thoughts may be deemed as positive or negative.

Different forms of education also play a major role in personal responsibility as well as the development of your character. Some find they are quick learners, while others not so, but in trying to become the best you can be, under-achievement or even unfulfilled potential does not exist.

※ ※ ※

Be able to hold your head high; not with ego or pride, but in the knowledge your self-esteem and good character are worth their weight in 'spiritual gold'.

Realise you can access and utilise the riches of the cosmos within; while the exterior 'you' that people view (perhaps with closed hearts), maybe one of a pauper.

Therefore, physical appearances can be deceptive, but when you listen to what resonates inside, you find the truth. In fact, this will guide you as your body ages, and when the weeks, months and years feel like they pass by in no time at all.

Your Physical and Non-Physical Journey

The stages of your life may be governed by colour, race, language, fame or fortune and the shape and size of the body ... but whatever your condition and wherever you find yourself, recall the unique opportunity I have empowered within you.

You can make your ultimate dream a reality. No 'man', institution, government, or any earthly power can withhold you from me, because I love you, and we will be together forever.

True vision occurs when your heart and mind and soul are in unison, and this will reveal your own path before you, with a signpost of truth for every turn and junction of your lives.

Can you see these with physical eyes alone? The answer, of course, is no. Would you ask the partially blind, surrounded by dense fog, to view an object on the horizon?

In times of trials and tribulations, the illusory mist of confusion can descend upon your clear thinking to frustrate and hinder and make you believe you are stuck, rooted to the spot, unable to see your hand in front of your face.

The calmest decision would then be to wait, keep still, and draw on your Divine essence within you... for inside what you call the body is 'I', the constant witness and spark of light more powerful than your mind could ever imagine.

You can live in a mansion, but you can only fall asleep in one bed. Some though, assume bigger is better and this is fine if true reasons exist behind those thoughts and wishes.

It is vital however to remove attachments, wherever and whenever possible in all that is said and done. This becomes simple when you lose the sense of a 'what is mine is mine' attitude or the debilitating want of the 'more' syndrome.

In fact, by becoming detached emotionally from the material elements of the impermanent world, a smoother road lies ahead.

Try to eradicate sentiment, for, like cement, it attempts to bind you. In doing so, the false attachment is removed and 'sent-to-me' instead. I retain it as my burden, and not your own because you no longer need to rely upon it. You will begin to acknowledge the freedom in your life, this I assure you.

❋ ❋ ❋

The world needs to understand every person, community and country is equal, so how can any life be more precious in the West or the East? Are those who live north of the equator more important than those in the south?

You all need each other in far greater ways than you imagine. This is not just in commerce, but also in real terms of creating peace and harmony. This will happen only through trust and friendship, and not in trying to impose the will of one over another.

❋ ❋ ❋

As dawn breaks and the Sun rises in the phenomenal world, the light brings warmth and substance to all living things. Similarity, the illumination of your heart and soul radiates and reflects all you are, all that you have been, and all that will become. In accordance with Universal law and memory, your whole being can reveal these in the form of human, beastly or Godly actions and qualities.

※ ※ ※

You can stay grounded, safe, and secure, in the understanding that your faith and trust may sometimes waver but will not be broken. At the same time, you are growing and reaching upwards to the light, towards greater frequencies and resonance of my love.

Each morning can be a blessing or a curse, depending on your perspective and outlook. Please look for and retain the joyful aspects of your new day and those opportunities to shine from inside your soul.

※ ※ ※

Once awake, are you grateful for your sleep and for the ability to rise from your bed?

When you opened your eyes, how much gratitude do you have for being able to see the alarm clock, while there are others without sight? And as you dress, putting on extra clothes for warmth on a cold winter's day, can you spare a thought for those who walk half-naked upon their own road and journey of experience?

Your Physical and Non-Physical Journey

Contemplate this too, when you wash your face and clean your teeth with fresh water (perhaps leaving the tap running), does a notion trickle down from the mind and into your heart, for those who pray for a single sip to quench their thirst?

✣ ✣ ✣

When you make the commitment to continually step forward towards the light, your perception of life within and around you will change beyond recognition. In fact, living with true insight can provide new meaning to your future and a real purpose to exist … or, for all that's said and done, you may still decide to stay upon the same course as you imagine you are at this present time.

✣ ✣ ✣

Comprehend that you must endeavour to become selfless, not selfish. Be thoughtful, not thoughtless. Be kind, and not blind to another's emotions or heart.

Each person deserves to be happy (and can be), but problems occur when you believe someone is not being how you want them to be.

Guard against this, for one's mind will yearn

to control everyone and anything, which can soon become second nature. This is wrong ... as you are all free to be 'you', and the best person you can be.

� ✦ ✦

Love is uncomplicated, being simple in its manifestation of, from and throughout all Creation. If followed, it is the one path which will never lead you astray or into disarray. It is the beacon of truth, a perpetual flame just like the spark of Divinity within your heart's centre.

It does not need any man-made method to light the way ahead for no street lamps are required to see where you are going... your own pathway is already lit, if you can trust all is as it should be.

✦ ✦ ✦

During your earthbound days, please dismiss irritable circumstances or situations like a fly buzzing around the room and landing upon you... consider it no more than a minor inconvenience.

Ask yourself, how do you react in such times? And, do you let another's habits consume your attention and waking hours? Is it possible for you to rise above someone else's traits or behaviour, accepting them as no more than mirroring your own?

Throughout your current embodiment, it is natural to look for (and take) the so-called easier route, attempting to evade life's pitfalls in the belief it can somehow bring you more quickly (and even closer) to me.

But whatever you believe, please comprehend there are so many roads and pathways in Creation. This is why your sojourn is often called the 'pathless' path ... because each provides a 'choice-less' choice. The only question now is, "When will you start to become who you are meant to be?"

All the accolades and success bestowed by one person to another, or even by society in general, are all by-products of life. They will all become distant memories and hence form the 'yesterdays' ... unlike love which is forever glorified and polished by my grace.

Therefore, by striving and in living to be the best human being you can be—with truth, nonviolence, kindness, peace, joy and most of all love—the exterior trappings of earthly success, whether this is through fame and fortune, or health and friendships, will all individually (or collectively) fall upon the eternal road you take.

※ ※ ※

Your soul retains the capacity to realise its true potential, though latent abilities can remain suppressed and withdrawn due to a loss of innocence, and the stress and decay of one's thoughts, words, and deeds.

As such, the road to enlightenment, bliss and a permanent state of being can be as easy or as difficult as you make it. The source of your difficulties lies not in others, but in the 'self' and self-denial.

※ ※ ※

Please also consider your emotions, regarding the attachment and desire for towards possessions and everything else in the material, transient world, for you cannot keep them with you.

They are mere 'trinkets' and all become irrelevant in the grander scheme of things, as only your love and divine essence of the soul endures. In fact, you may work your fingers to the bone and accumulate property, money and all manner of luxuries, but as mentioned before, they can help you exist, but they do not teach or show you how to live.

'Class' comes not from ownership or upon the standard of your journey, but in what you do and complete within it, so always keep this in mind.

※ ※ ※

A person could flick a light switch or turn the central heating on, lay their head upon a soft pillow, place shoes on their feet, retain money in their pockets, wear a coat on their back and have food and water in their stomach, yet still remain dissatisfied.

Realise, this is not a guilt trip to be self-induced or enforced upon the reader or listener, but a reminder of one's contentment, attachments, and gratitude on their path of life.

※ ※ ※

Do not fear what people call fate, or even what you think might be lost, stolen, or taken away from your life, because it is only attachments which bring anxiety, a lack of contentment and distrust.

Instead, move forward to share the true you, so the future days of your journey and diary become the permanent record and legacy of your Divinity; whereby your character and personality glow from each page, helping other souls who cross your path, or those that join you on the road of truth.

When you walk in truth, you do not need to worry where you tread, as the pathway across the emotional waters of your existence remains strong and greatly enhanced, leading you onward and forwards to endless bliss and peace.

And when you place your feet, your kindness will grip and gently guide you one step at a time, to cross over those pools of emotions with dryer eyes … no outpouring of ego or tears of sadness fuelled by frustration, worry or fear.

One may believe your future seems unknown, but this very day sustains and creates it. Each second and hour of life provides you with the opportunity to steadily move into the reality of

Your Physical and Non-Physical Journey

your own glory and Divine essence, or one can remain frozen, resembling a broken wristwatch or clock.

No matter what you face, whatever pain or heartache you seem to go through, the experience is fleeting compared to our infinite connection.

Of course, I do witness hurtful times. Many examples include your heart becoming emotionally drained from the believed loss of a loved one ... and when the 'body' feels broken through fear, anger, crime, and war.

The same occurs if the mind appears to snap from a lack of support or forgiveness; or if the soul's light of a thousand suns is covered and cast under a shadow of past deeds, regrets or failed dreams.

But know that this is when I hold your hand or whisper in your ear, and I am the seeds of positive thought that you can sense when you wade through the clutter of this impermanent world in which your physical now resides. So, keep strong and do not fade, not when you are so close to living the truth of all things.

A Pocket Full of God

People often want a quick and simple explanation, "Why don't you just tell us how to solve our problems?" Please be aware, your lives are the continuous result of your own actions (whether past, present, or future), and they contain your own lessons to understand and grow.

Imagine yourself in a school classroom, how much would you learn if the answers were already on the blackboard? Therefore, be strong in the knowledge I will never leave you. How can you be alone if I reside within your heart and you in mine?

In all your endeavour's, please shy away from self-criticism, for it is more often the case that no one else is judging you other than yourself. "He (or she) is more successful, fitter, slimmer, better looking, has fewer problems, and is luckier than I am." Are you so sure about these things?

Although it is sometimes difficult to count your blessings in the society in which you live today... it is vital you do so.

Your Physical and Non-Physical Journey

By offering a neighbour your hand of friendship, this vibrancy can expand between each home, village and town, and all cities, nations, and continents of the world… to build a new Eden and paradise of love.

Effort, determination, trust, and faith will play their part, but inside one's heart resides a clear road towards bliss and peace for yourself and all humanity.

Life is full of twists, turns, opportunities and openings, with choices and dreams from the cradle to the grave, so do not look back into the past with regrets. You cannot change it. Likewise, the future is only the seeds sown in the present.

Please do this with love and care in the ploughed furrows of truth inside your heart, in the knowledge they will grow and flourish there because my love will radiate upon them. Know that the foundation of your ambitions become nourished and sustained, by the fountain of tears from my joy.

Try not to let those old shadows of doubt creep and stretch from the corners of the mind. They only hide the way forward, disguising a smoother path ahead of you.

Instead, aim to use your creativity and intellect ... for I am the pen, pencil, paint, paper, and the canvass and so much more. Therefore, I ask you to utilise me in every way by thought, word and deed.

I am always here to help you, however, it is important to know that your spiritual growth comes through awareness, knowledge and subsequent wisdom, which provides you with what you need, rather than what you think you want.

✵ ✵ ✵

When faced with so-called difficulties, do not frown or despair. No matter what you do or where you are, if you are trying your best please forgive yourself.

Likewise, forgiving others will also help release them from their own bondage of misgivings and mistrust. You can do this if you try, whether it is through encouraging words, an arm around a shoulder, a smile or helping hand; for each is an act which stems from one heart to another.

Your Physical and Non-Physical Journey

Do not wish for easier paths or roads, but except the here and now and shine as brightly as possible, whatever comes your way. Realise you must treat the so-called good and bad, your ups and downs and likes and dislikes with equanimity.

As your journey continues, you may believe you are alone but never are, for even in your darkest hour I am with you. And though you often view your experiences as a hindrance, try to live your days in the knowledge that I bless you with my grace and love, and will always aid and guide you on many levels of your existence.

Determination is a key factor in your perception and spiritual development. Know there are many roads littered with failed aspirations, while hopes and dreams park in the recesses of the mind, just like vehicles stopped in their tracks … having run out of fuel.

This reduction of energy might be tiredness or simply an absence of will power. The first is easily remedied with rest, relaxation, and a decrease of stress in your life, whereas the second forms part of your character, which may be more difficult to change if a change is required.

※ ※ ※

Rather than seeking bigger rewards than that which you deserve (because of your ego), feel the goodness which shines back towards you. This has a greater value than any precious stone or ring of gold that 'man' can possess.

※ ※ ※

Remember, no ritual can ever be performed, nor any monument built, that could match the gift of love that you share both freely and truthfully as you make your way through life.

※ ※ ※

Try not to worry when things appear to go wrong, or if you fall, say that you cannot get back up again ... because such a hurdle could be the last one you ever need to overcome.

And, should you imagine your life as unbearable, think of me, trust me, and retain your faith in me too. Nothing is insurmountable. Allow me to help you, for I will carry all your burdens.

Your Physical and Non-Physical Journey

So, it is time to pick up the sword of truth and march forward into your destiny. The ego must be slain; cut into two, so that compassion and forgiveness not only shine forth but also remain behind, to reside within those memories and hearts where you have been.

Those footsteps will not fade and disappear as if walking on sand, but instead, they will leave an unending trace, becoming examples of how to 'walk' in joy for countless souls to follow.

There is so much for you to be positive about … because you have the ability to shine how your light is supposed to. If you can simply 'be' in the world but not become part of it, you gain true strength from within … both resolute and determined to alleviate the doubt and anxiety which may come your way.

Recognise the real beauty inside you too, and this will manifest around the globe, so try to fulfil your potential, and not waste the time that has been pre-sent to you.

A Pocket Full of God

You are beyond 'rich in Spirit' (and so much more), for a soul's illumination is brighter than a thousand suns.

I also urge you not to accept anyone else's truth, only what you feel is yours, and in following your own, be rest assured that no matter what road or path you take, it still leads and returns you back to me.

It is important you remember to retain faith in this, and even more so in yourself, for therein lies 'me', the answer to all things. I love you, so how could this not be so?

As I am you and you are me (the light, the way, and the truth), then you must start to see your future through different lenses.

Many will state that an ambition, goal, or the desire for reality is like looking through rose-tinted glasses … this is not the case, for if you look to, from and through your heart, you bear witness to the victory of all battles, which is over 'Self'.

Your Physical and Non-Physical Journey

Your journey should resemble an open book, so let these snippets of text reflect the same and carry you forward, as it is a never-ending story. As such, you are writing your own history every day, and may each become permanent markers and indicators of just how far you have grown as a human being and soul.

When the end of the road is reached and the goal attained … the aspirant, the devotee, the seeker of truth and the pilgrim will realise they have travelled only from their self to their self.

Afterword

Remember, what you read from any book or hear from a guide, sage or guru are just guidelines and advice, and they may not be something you fully agree with or convinced by.

However, the world around you can only reflect what the 'I'—your true 'self'—makes of it. So, do you choose to imagine further pain, fear, hate and a desire for self-preservation (which resides outside of you) or will you rise above self-doubt and ego to exude kindness, peace and joy through the expansion from within?

Whatever you decide, please understand that there is nothing wrong with how you wish to live … but why remain limited? If you can just try to relate and experiment with the process of turning inward—beyond the boundary of the senses—you will become more conscious of reality every day.

With an new awareness of everything you currently cling to, one's own perception and experiences of the depths and dimensions of the boundless will ultimately lead to vitality of the body, a joyful mind and a loving heart, which will then enable you to live a full and blissful life … and who doesn't want that?

Bibliography

Here is a selection of my favourite books. The list is a merely a sample of literature available in the Mind, Body and Spirit / Spiritual / Self-Help section at libraries, local bookshops and online. I hope you will enjoy reading them too!

A Course in Miracles
By the Foundation for Inner Peace.
ISBN 0-670-86975-9

A Mind of your Own
By Betty Shine
ISBN 0-00-255894-7-0

Anastasia - The Ringing Cedar series - Book 1
By Vladimir Megre
ISBN 978-0-9801812-0-3

Angels Inspiration
By Diana Cooper
ISBN 0-340-7332-3

A Pocket Full of God

A Walk with Jesus – Enjoying the company of Christ.
By R.C. Sproul
ISBN 978-1857-922608

Conversations with God
By Neale Donald Walsh
Book 1 - ISBN 0-340-69325-8
Book 2 - ISBN 0-340-76544-5
Book 3 - ISBN 0-340-76545-3

Confessions of a Pilgrim
By Paulo Coelho
ISBN 0-7225-3293-8

Chicken Soup for the Soul
By Jack Canfield and Mark Victor Hansen
ISBN 0-09185-428-8

Embraced by the Light – What happens when we die?
By Betty J. Eadie
ISBN 1-85538-4116

How Sai Baba Attracts Without Direct Contact – Diary of a 21st Century Devotee
By Dr Tommy. S.W. Wong
ISBN 1-4486-0416-8

Bibliography

Lessons from the Source: A Spiritual
Guidebook for Navigating Life's Journey
By Jack Armstrong
ISBN 0-615-86984-X

Life after Death – The case for survival of
bodily death.
By D Scott Rogo
ISBN 0-8530-504-7

Sai Baba Gita-
The Way to Self-Realization and Liberation in
this age
By Al Drucker
ISBN 0-9638449-0-3

Signposts
By Denise Linn
ISBN 0-7126-749-7

The Bible Code
By Michael Drosnin
ISBN 0-297-82994-7

The Celestine Prophecy- An Adventure
By James Redfield
ISBN 0-533-40902-6

A Pocket Full of God

The Complete Book of Dreams
By Edwin Raphael
ISBN 0-572-01714-6

The Day my life changed
By Carmel Reilly
ISBN 978-1-84509-420-1

The Garden of the Golden Flower – The Journey to Spiritual Fulfilment
By Longfield Beatty
ISBN 1-85958-15- X

The Infinite Boundary
By Guy Lyon Playfair
ISBN 0-285-622048

The Message of a Master
By John McDonald
ISBN 0-931432-952

The Path to Love
By Deepak Chopra
ISBN 0-7126-7224-9

The Winds of Change
By Stephanie J. King
ISBN 978-0-95421-6-9

Bibliography

Universe Has Your Back: Transform Fear to Faith
By Gabrielle Bernstein
ISBN 1-4019-4654-8

About the Author

David has helped to conduct Spiritual Development and healing circles for over 25 years. He has also been a guest speaker—sharing his enlightened experiences to promote 'oneness' and self-realisation—at various Mind, Body and Spirit engagements across the UK.

Through visualisations, inner-dictation, dream interpretation, meditation, mindfulness, pre-cognition and healing, the books he co-writes with 'Spirit' provide the foundation to discover your own path of truth.

With a renewed sense of purpose, the Spiritual Guidance and Education directs the seeker to become 'realised', whereby you perceive what is already there … the truth within the permanence of life-energy and love. David is tee-total and a vegetarian, who loves the sunshine, nature, animals, and his wife!

Glossary – Spiritual Guidance and Education

Abundance: Awaken your consciousness, to the knowingness of your own creative abundant energy, a part of creation.

Affirmations: Help us to purify our thoughts and restructure the dynamic of our brains. Personal affirmations are positive, specific sentences which need to be in the present tense, often repeated several times to encourage or motivate yourself. The word affirmation comes from Latin 'affimare', originally meaning "to make steady, strengthen."

Amen: A Hebrew word that means "so be it". Usually said at the end of a prayer, we are asking God, "Please let it be as we have prayed". NB. When people place their hands/palms together it signifies a negative and positive flow of energy. The left receives and the right sends. The same hand gesture is a customary Hindu and Buddhist greeting called Namaste but is also used when leave-taking too.

It is sometimes spoken as Namaskar or Namaskaram.

Angel: The word "angel" is derived from the Greek word angelos which means 'messenger'. They are divine spirits, each of God's consciousness and these beings of light intercede for us, answering our prayers and calls for help.

Archangel: Hierarchs (leaders) of the Angels.

Ascension: Is the process whereby the soul, (having balanced /removed karma and fulfilled its Divine plan) merges first with the Universal /Christ Consciousness and then with the living presence of the I AM THAT I AM. Once the Ascension has taken place, the soul becomes a permanent atom of the 'Body of God'. Please remember, your ascension is not something you plan for or takes place on a certain date. You are actively choosing a process to evolve into higher consciousness ... through expanded awareness and integrating the higher reverberation of your spiritual self. So, the act of ascending; is to climb to a greater plane/dimension which involves total transformation on all levels (all that you are) ... realigned with Divine love.

Glossary – Spiritual Guidance and Education

In Christian belief, the ascent of Jesus Christ into Heaven on the 40th day after his resurrection ... his return to sit on the right-hand side of the 'Father'.

Astral Projection: A breaking free by the astral 'body', believed to occur just before death or during some dreams. Also known as out-of-body experience (OBE).

Assumptions: You must remove all assumptions. Children are getting 'raised' and many of their parent's beliefs are being superimposed upon them. But how can anyone perceive 'God'/Creator/life-energy when they do not even understand the full nature of 'existence'? Do not assume anything ... you only need to experience it.

Atma: The Soul, Universal Consciousness.

Aum: This is the Universal, sacred, and indestructible sound. The frequency of the same word that went forth as the origin of creation ... the basis and root of all sounds of your existence. By sounding the AUM comes our oneness and can provide many benefits to the body and mind. It is a spiritual process unaffected by culture or language and is the pathway to how your energies function. Each letter stands for a component of our divinity and is intended to be sounded separately ... with repetition and great awareness as the reverberation flows within you, moving from the navel to the tip of your nose. (Remember to pronounce the letters as Aa's, Ooo's and Mmm's). The A comes forth from Alpha (our Father) as the initiator, the creator, the beginning of consciousness of being ... the thrust of power. The M is the is the OM (our Mother) the conclusion/ending... one with the Holy Spirit–therefore the positive and negative polarities of being are pronounced. From the A to the Om, all the vastness of creation is contained and so the U in the centre is the cup cradling you (the centre piece)—the real self in universal manifestation—so, A-U-M is the Trinity in unity. In the East, Hindus refer to the Trinity as Brahma, Vishnu, and Shiva ... the relevant forces of Creation, Maintenance and Destruction. In the West... the Trinity is Father, Son, and the Holy Spirit. NB. The meaning in Sanskrit is "I bow, I agree, I accept". I bow before God Almighty, I agree that I am the 'son', and I accept my immortal destiny.

Aura: An invisible emanation or field of energy believed to radiate from a person or object.

Glossary – Spiritual Guidance and Education

Auric Field: Your chakra system, subtle bodies and other subtle energy points create an interconnecting field of energy around the physical body.

Awareness: Is vital to your progress as a seeker to connect with your divine nature. Therefore, you must become aware of the external chatter which detracts from your inner enquiry. Do not just 'observe' but give your full attention to your consciousness—not the body and mind. And, it will help if you only focus on one activity at a time … so do not multitask. This way, divinity will manifest through you! Remember, the less you do, the less personality is involved and the more 'aware' of life you become.

Balance: We know that karma is action, and all your experiences of joy, misery, happiness, and suffering happen within you. Once you have truly grasped the fact that this encompasses your entire system of mind, body, soul, and energy, it can be the springboard to finding true balance. This becomes easier if you don't let the mind work against you … a necessity to experience the Divinity and bring brilliance into your life. So, try to attain this through every aspect your physicality, your diet, thoughts, sleep, posture and breathing … everything!

Bliss/blissful: This is not a goal or attainment in itself. You need to make it your purpose, the foundation and way of your life. Everything else plays out from this.

Body: The vessel (some call it a shell, overcoat, or even a bubble) which houses our senses through which we perceive everything. The physical body is also shaped by our evolutionary and genetic memory. It thrives or withers by the food we eat, inherited from Mother Earth, and nourished by Creation. In addition, it allows the faith and goodwill of the Divine intent.

Bondage: What we have created for ourselves materialises from nothing more than our likes and dislikes. Bondage also refers to the identification we have placed upon our bodies and minds, and not with people, places, or material/physical objects. It all lies in your mind … your thoughts. One who considers themselves free becomes free. One who considers themselves bound remains bound. So, you are what you think and therefore if you think you are just body and mind you are … if you think you are boundless you are! Ironically, use your thoughts to go beyond the bondage of your thoughts! Remember, there is no bondage in consciousness.

Causal body: The highest and innermost 'body' which veils the Atma/soul. A doorway to higher consciousness.

Chakras: The Chakra 'system' is a vital part of our mental, emotional, physical, and spiritual 'bodies'. There are 112 funnel-shaped energy points within… and 2 'outside' of us.

Consciousness: Intellect without memory … pure and unsullied by the mind's impressions and body experiences.

Compassion: A frequency of Divine love coming from the soul through the heart chakra.

Death: The important aspect here is that you must experience to 'know'. Therefore, one has to acknowledge what you do or do not know, and what you believe or disbelieve too. Death is fiction, death is life, death is a continuation. When the body dies it has become unsustainable for life (your soul), so the conscious mind moves on, retaining all qualities bar discrimination. We need to relate this to karma yet again, for it acts like a bubble retaining the soul within the body. Imagine the bubble has burst and the air within now merges with totality, and so becomes enlightened.

Decrees: Relate to the science of the spoken word. A step up from all prayer forms both East and West, they combine prayer, meditation, and visualisation, and place a special emphasis on affirmations using the name of God—I AM THAT I AM. An effective method in balancing karma, spiritual resolution, and soul advancement.

Destiny: People often blame a negative outcome as a result of their so-called destiny, but in doing so they place a total limitation upon their life and so cannot be free. However, it is you (and only you) who makes your life!

Devotion: All forms of devotion arise from your emotions. It provides you with a sense of freedom and comes from the heart... unlike belief, which materialises from the mind. It is what is devoid of 'you' ... and allows grace to flow through you. One may experience this by allowing a greater intelligence to work through you whilst keeping your intellect at bay.

Glossary – Spiritual Guidance and Education

Divinity: The state or quality of being Divine.

Earth-plane: The world of material form.

East and West: East is often related to the destruction of all that is unreal... and the purification of the veil of Maya (illusion) by Lord Shiva. West is usually termed with the action of the Holy Spirit.

Ego: The ego is the unconscious/lower self and it only identifies with the body and mind. However, in truth this lower self does not really exist … it is only an absence of awareness, just like darkness which is the absence of light. So, one cannot be aware of and also ecstatic/blissful at the same time. In contrast, your reality is the infinite or higher self ... pure intelligence. Remember, you do not need to 'see' to identify with the all 'knowing', and when you remove the ego you are able to experience pure joy.

Enlightenment: Everything is lit up; you see the reality of life/existence. True insight and comprehension.

Etheric Body: This is the body charged by God with the holy memory of all things lovely and beautiful within the substance of the Divine world … in order that you may bask in that power which one day you will know to its fullest.

Experience: Only by turning inward can you discover bliss and liberation and true peace of the Divine. You must experience it yourself, and this will not happen by reading a book, traveling somewhere, or when you listen to any other human being.

Food: There is a direct correlation with your dietary habits and sleep. The greater amount you consume requires more energy by the body (especially during sleep) to process it … hence the more tired you can feel. While the body needs food to survive, this has no relation to social or religious background. If you were truly starving and there was a choice of a plate of food and God's presence to appear in front of you, what would you choose to partake/digest? Your self-preservation will kick in! However, the amount you eat on a daily basis is compulsive or conscious in nature. Will you, therefore, embrace this freedom of choice or have you become a slave to this requirement? As the world endures the COVID-19 pandemic it has been scientifically proven that those who are obese have less ability to overcome the virus. The morals and ethics of how we look after our bodies (with food intake and exercise) can be encapsulated in the question … "How long do we want to live?" To help further, understand that different food can be full of positive, negative, or contain no 'pranic' (life-energy) at all … which leads to lethargy. Some foods like Honey (with hot water) are so good they break down fat, others dull your nervous system or may stop your bodies sensitivity too. The digestion of everything inside your stomach has various timescales. For example, most fruit takes about 3 hours, whereas meat could take 2-3 days! If you could imagine a piece of meat left in the hot sun for the same time it would fester and become full of bacteria. Inside you, the bodies temperature creates the same conditions, so once again the choice to have something like this (rotting flesh) inside you remains. Ideally, your diet should contain at least 40% of fruit, vegetables, nuts etcetera. After eating, the most advantageous proportions inside your stomach would be for it to contain 1/2 full, 1/4 water, 1/4 empty.

Forbearance: An important quality indeed. The spiritual seeker must appreciate that happiness in their life occurs by totally trusting in the universe and remaining in an acceptance mode.

This way, one's joy and peace will always remain undisturbed and you will never feel frustrated, impatient, or let down.

Forgiveness: Is the key to connect with the open door of your own Christ-self. The quality of love is all-encompassing and all-forgiving. Learn to forgive others and most of all yourself, for true healing.

Free-will: The discretion to use or not use … the freedom of 'choice'. The question then arises over how much of your life unfolds automatically or compulsively (if it is not happening the way you want it to) rather than acting with your intelligence … consciously.

Glory: Recognise the glory of your own soul, your divine link with the glory of God, Creator, Universal intelligence. See and feel its glorious reflection within yourself.

Grace: Receiving God's grace can be automatic, but usually follows the effort and endeavour made by the 'seeker'. It requires non-resistance and unconditional acceptance in the reality of our oneness and boundless state.

Guru: 'Gu' means darkness, 'ru' means

dispeller. Therefore, a Guru is someone who dispels darkness … to throw light on your very nature of existence.

Happiness: To be happy you must stop finding fault with anything and everything … situations, people, and things. One must surrender to the acceptance of what is because true happiness has no cause behind it. To experience this, you must know yourself by removing all dependence on external situations… which allows you to discover the true 'uncaused' happiness of your real nature—bliss.

Heart: Your heart is a gift from creation. It is the seat of your soul and the very altar of God. Comprehend that inside the heart there is a central chamber, surrounded and protected by a forcefield known as the 'cosmic interval'. This chamber is separated from Matter, and no microscope or probing can ever discover it. Only true vision—when the eyes of the body, soul and mind are in unison can one bear witness to its magnificence. Know that it is the connecting point of the powerful crystal cord of light that descends from your God presence—which sustains the beating of your physical heart. This also gives your life purpose and a reason for integration with the cosmos. Therefore, we must cherish this contact point of 'life' by turning within to pay conscious recognition to it.

Healing: Is a letting-go process… do it every day as you hold and welcome love into your heart. Every day you have the power to express the light of your Divinity to any life who needs it. Know that the healing process takes place first in the soul—spiritually and emotionally. Then the mind, mentally and visually … followed by the body, which will always reflect the state of your true and higher self.

Higher Self: A person's spiritual self, their true identity … a focus to many meditation techniques, as opposed to the physical body.

Human being: A definition which defines us. Our consciousness and intellect distinguish us from all other life forms because we know 'how to be'.

I: Most people—when saying 'I'—are referring to (or thinking of) their body or mind, however 'I' represents 'Immortal consciousness'.

I AM: You are saying "God in me is" … so that

everything you say after these words manifests in our world.

I AM THAT I AM: The name and living presence of 'God' the 'as above so below'. In the West—the path of the Mother—descends. In the East, "OM TAT SAT OM"—the path of the Spirit—ascends. The energy of your being and all that is locked in imperfection becomes a spiral of the ascension and returns to the heart of the God presence.

Identity: Your true identity is part of the cosmos. You have to shift from what the mind believes is just the physical, to that of consciousness. Without the light, your identity is like a moth drawn to and darting around the flame of truth … but charring or burning your wings to depart into the abyss of suffering and darkness … without having attained illumination and liberation.

Inspiration: One of the greatest gifts of your Divinity is to become the example, the inspiration whereby you move from 'unwillingness' to 'willingness'. God provides you with droplets of truth, those golden nuggets of wisdom, the fragments of creation to stimulate your thoughts and actions to 'create'.

Even if you feel that you have not reached the pinnacle, or conversely feel like you have plummeted to the depths … you retain the ability inside you to inspire.

Invocation: The act or instance of invoking, a prayer or command to a higher power, deity, spirit, God for assistance, Divine guidance, forgiveness, and protection. Sometimes used in the opening of a religious festival. It is also a way of bringing the best out in you.

Journey: The most important journey you can undertake in this lifetime is from being unconscious to conscious. This includes your thoughts, words and deeds and everything within and around you!

Joy: Try to bring a feeling of lightness to your heart and a renewed joy in living. Laughter and joyous love will bring out the child in you, transmuting any feelings of negativity and heaviness within you. Make your days joyful and watch the world around change for the better!

Karma: Literally means 'Action' and is of your own making. Most of your actions are unconscious, played out through one's physical, mental, emotional and life-energy. Also believed to be the totality of a person's actions and conduct and memory during successive incarnations or regarded as cause and effect that may influence their destiny. Karma is also considered to be a law or principle through which such influence is believed to operate … fate resulting from one's previous actions. However, counteracting a 'fate/destiny' scenario, it is incredibly empowering to know that each day is our own making. Misery or joy are the choice which affects the very nature of our lives. Therefore, you are responsible for your own future … it is in your own hands!

Light: The highest frequency we know. Your physical eyes can only see that which is stopped by light. However, the pure element of the 'I' bears witness to all creation because it sees without being tarnished by memory, and views everything exactly the way it is. Jesus once said, "The light of the body is eye (I). If therefore thine eye (I) be single, thy whole body shall be full of light."

Logic: Try not to get bogged down or become a slave to logic and the reasoning/propositions and conclusions of others. Validate the truth of your reality through your own experiences, for the cosmos is here and now!

Love: Love is the way you are. Love enables us to fulfil the destiny of the soul in conscious outer manifestation—a just and merciful compassion that is always rewarded by individual creative fulfilment. Through the power of love, man learns how they may impart into others the beauty and compassion that they have received from God. Love does not need to have sustenance from anyone, therefore, if you are loving … it spreads!

Mantra: A word or formula (often in Sanskrit). They attune you and govern the release or attraction of life-energy, which becomes deposited in your aura. This expands over time, gaining momentum. For example, this powerful mantra from India "OM NANORA RIJA NIYA" tunes oneself with the infinite. "O infinite God, I want your will to be done in me".

Meditation: Practiced for millennia, and originally intended to develop spiritual understanding, awareness, and direct experience of ultimate reality. Although an important spiritual practice in many religions and traditions, it can be practiced regardless of someone's religious or cultural background. It can be used with other forms of medical treatment, and as a complementary therapy for the many stress-related conditions. Types of meditation include concentration, movement, mindfulness, and transcendental. When you meditate you are just withdrawing support from your personality, you are creating a distance between your true self and your mind … in essence, observing from an elevated, clearer viewpoint.

Mind: Eastern philosophy and wisdom state there are 16 segments to the mind. The 4 main 'parts' relate to intellect, identity, memory (evolutionary and genetic) and pure intelligence. It encapsulates our thoughts and emotions. NB. People often refer to their 'monkey' mind during meditation, but our purpose is to liberate it, not control it!

Mindfulness: Reconnecting with our bodies, and the sensations they experience. Becoming aware of our thoughts and feelings through our senses—knowing what is going on inside and around ourselves—at any given moment.

Omnipotent: Having unlimited or Universal power, authority, or force; all-powerful.

Omnipresent: The state of being everywhere at once. All-pervading, Universal, ever-present.

Omniscient: Having total knowledge, knowing everything. All-knowing, all-seeing, wise.

Path: It does not matter what route you take if you are just constantly striving for 'more'. Know that you will never reach the destination if you continually require and crave more love, more money, more success etcetera. Only the pathless path brings you the perception, the clarity and the focus needed to liberate and experience perpetual bliss.

Patience: Recognise and feel the principle of patience to release tension in the mind and body and your life. With greater awareness, an increase in your level of endurance and ability to suffer restlessness and annoyance without complaint.

Personality: This is the one and the only real difference between each human being. It reflects and manifests as our likes and dislikes in every way and form imaginable … and thus induces bondage.

Purification: A high dimensional frequency

Glossary – Spiritual Guidance and Education

which can operate at a causal body level throughout the subtle bodies (mind, etheric, physical, and emotional), and the auric field. This transmutes lower energies and allows a new feeling of purity to filter through the conscious mind.

Responsibility: One could say this is our ability to respond to everything that occurs within and outside of us. In real terms, our ability to respond to any given situation is limitless, whereas our ability to act is limited. It is the simplest way to express our divinity too.

Self-realisation: The expression used in psychology, spirituality, and Eastern religions. Can be defined as the fulfilment by oneself of the possibilities of one's character, personality, potential and Divinity. To become 'realised' means you finally perceive what is already there! Please note … that the instruments of your perception are all outward bound, but the seat of experience is within you.

Senses: Nature has allowed you to live life through the sense organs. Eyes provide sight to beautiful scenes and all your surroundings. Ears enable sound and melody to soothe or stir your emotions. The nose permits the aroma and fragrances of creation to ignite your imagination. Taste enables you to savour nutritious food which give life and health to the body. Touch gives you the opportunity to know and feel personal contact. However, the common theme with each sense is that they all crave and desire … which only leads to your likes and dislikes creating bondage. You must, therefore, use your intelligence to control the mind and take charge of the senses for spiritual life. A true seeker will only become fulfilled this way to experience eternal bliss. NB. An old Indian metaphor captures this perfectly, "Use the intellect-charioteer to take charge of the reins of the mind and your sense-horses … if you want to reach the destination of Self-realisation".

Silence: Is that which is NOT the basis of sound. Keeping silent has an immensely powerful impact on your life … a representation of 'nothingness'. Many guides also state you should reduce what you say by 50% … and even my wife says I talk too much! Remember, silence is the speech of the spiritual seeker.

Sleep: It is well known that the body rejuvenates and even repairs itself during sleep, but whether the average human being requires 8 hours is debatable. Of course, there may be hormonal issues in play which affect the need for even more sleep too, but it is important to cut down on it. Try to arise after 5 or 6 hours, or at least as soon as you awake. This might seem difficult to action, but this may allow you to experience another 10 or more years of life! So, if by the alarm clock or by naturally waking with the dawn chorus, do not just turn over … thinking 'I love my bed', or that you cannot get up citing 'you need to recharge the batteries'. Know it is not so much physical rest you require but more the time to ease the restless mind to re-awaken the Divinity within you. Therefore, will you stand by your bed and gaze upon the imprint of your slumber? Will you continue to resist life's tasks and tests, or grasp the opportunities presenting themselves in a new day? Why not embrace your 'aliveness' to bring joy into your life and all those around you too? In reality, sleep is a death state which you enter into through instalments (inertia) whereas life is dynamic. Remember, you cannot 'enjoy' sleep, but to rest and the time for restfulness is the basis of all your activity.

Sojourn: A temporary stay; a brief period of residence.

Spirituality: Going beyond the boundary of the body/senses. You experience the reality past the physical presence, and in life, react with your intelligence consciously.

Spiritual seeker: Many people understand that being a seeker involves making a total and absolute surrender to 'life' by accepting whatever comes their way. However, when transformation, guidance, and the materialisation of what is sought does not occur… grave doubt may arise. Then, further obstacles or suffering will usually generate the question, "Why me?" or "Why is it happening?" But this only creates a further barrier, so it is crucial not to think or ask the 'why' question! If you can only transcend the need for any clarification in all your experiences (whether deemed 'good', 'bad', or indifferent) this will finally allow the Universal consciousness and life-energy to resolve the situation for your higher good and at the earliest opportunity too.

Stillness: Being still empowers you because it allows you to be in touch with another dimension. When you are consciously 'still', the energy you access becomes a link between the non-physical and physical elements of your existence … so you are able to witness the reality of life in its entirety. In essence, you leave your perception of a limited identity behind to see and experience the truth. Understand that stillness is not sleep, which is unconscious slumber.

Time: Seconds, minutes and hours are not your true pillars of existence. It is not how little or how much time you have, but what you do with it that counts. When you are joyful, time will seem to disappear, when you are miserable … a day can feel like eternity. When you turn inward and have no sense of body, you detach yourself from the clock face and the unreal develops into reality. When you truly accept the awareness and the inevitability of the 'moment', all suffering is gone. Understand everything in creation is in this moment, whereas your mind thinks of the future (imagination) and the past (memory). So, one must be conscious and live in the moment, for it is only this moment which is inevitable!

Turning inward: When you sit still in silence, there is an opportunity to 'experience' your reality beyond the senses. In doing so, what you have previously classed as your identity (which were bound by one's sex, race, religion, and beliefs), will break free and lose its limitations.

Transformation: Nothing of the old 'you' should remain—in contrast to improvement, which is just a 'change.' As such, the object of your desires may alter your destination, but only when you stop seeking/asking/striving for what you do not have can you change the inner process of one's life. By transformation, you shift oneself to a completely new dimension of perception and experience ... hence 'self-transformation'.

Tranquillity: When the subtle vibrations which surround the body become disturbed, you feel stressed. You need to combat this, so take the mind elsewhere. Visualise somewhere calm, perhaps by a still lake or a special place held dear to your heart. Allow peace to wash over you and bring tranquillity to your body, thoughts, and consciousness.

Truth: Can only be perceived and experienced, it cannot be interpreted.

Unconditional love: This form of love is not emotional and has no strings or ties. It is the only true healing power, so try to allow your heart to be activated in this way.

Vibration and energy: The resonance of your

true 'self'. We are all at different stages of spiritual development, so the intensity of reverberation (sound) within would indicate the energy level you have reached. Every substance has its own frequency, its own keynote. Every sound has form and every form has sound.

Visualisation: A mental image, like one's visual perception.

Wisdom: 'Wise dominion' … wisdom to nourish the mind—for illumination and the right use of the knowledge of Universal law.

Yoga: A group of physical, mental, and spiritual practices or disciplines which originated in ancient India. One of six Astika schools of Hindu philosophical traditions. In the West, it is often seen as just bending of the body, for a better posture or exercise … but in the East, it is a contemporary science, vitally relevant to our times.

An invitation from David Knight

Receive a free e-book when you join David's mission for a 'full and blissful life'.

To learn more, visit
https://www.ascensionforyou.com

An Invitation from David Knight

Follow us on Facebook:
https://facebook.com/AscensionForYou

or Twitter:
https://twitter.com/ascensionforyou

… and become part of our community who love to receive uplifting messages for the heart and soul!

Want to let others know what you think? Please make your opinion known by leaving a 'star rating' with one-click on Amazon.com or Amazon.co.uk and/or a review at your favorite online retailer.

Thank you!

www.ingramcontent.com/pod-product-compliance
Lightning Source LLC
LaVergne TN
LVHW021714060526
838200LV00050B/2654